Somewhere Over the Rainbow

Also by Daniel Ross Goodman

Novels
A Single Life

Edited Books
Black Fire on White Fire: Essays in Honor of Rabbi Avi Weiss

Somewhere Over the Rainbow

*Wonder and Religion
in American Cinema*

Daniel Ross Goodman

Hamilton Books
Lanham • Boulder • New York • Toronto • London

Published by Hamilton Books
An imprint of The Rowman & Littlefield Publishing Group, Inc.
4501 Forbes Boulevard, Suite 200, Lanham, Maryland 20706
Hamilton Books Acquisitions Department (301) 459-3366

6 Tinworth Street, London SE11 5AL, United Kingdom

British Library Cataloguing in Publication Information Available

Library of Congress Cataloging Data Available

ISBN 978-0-7618-7223-8 (pbk. : alk. paper)
ISBN 978-0-7618-7224-5 (electronic)

♾TM The paper used in this publication meets the minimum requirements of American National Standard for Information Sciences Permanence of Paper for Printed Library Materials, ANSI/NISO Z39.48-1992.

לע״נ
In Loving Memory of Rabbi Neil Gillman

הרב נחום בן יצחק הכהן ורבקה גילמן
"We discover God. We invent the metaphors."

For
Daniel Epstein, Seth Herstic, and Jonathan Leener

MAIORUM NUGAE NEGOTIA VOCANTUR, PUERORUM AUTEM
TALIA CUM SINT, PUNIUNTUR A MAIORIBUS.

The idling of our elders is called business, the idling of boys, though quite
like it, is punished by those same elders . . .

—Augustine, *Confessions*

Contents

Foreword

Movies can provide escapist entertainment that dumbs down the mind and passes the time into oblivion. They can also connect us to the transcendent, fill our lives with existential meaning or lead us to search for the depths of being. In this book, Daniel Goodman opens our eyes to the spiritual feast available for the taking in films.

Under cover of reviewing movies, Goodman leads us on a journey to meaning and inspiration. For the religious searcher, he breaks us out of the narrow box of canonical literature and leads us to browse in the enchanted forest of movies. For the spiritually inert, he awakens us to go beneath the surface of life and allows films to enable us to see the world with new eyes.

This is a serious book but it is fun to read. On page after page, it surprises us with new insights drawn out of old iconic screen moments. After reading Goodman, you will reverse the old adage. Instead of saying "I lost it at the movies," you will say: "I found it (vision/divinity/global connectivity) at the movies." Thank God and thank Goodman.

Rabbi Irving (Yitz) Greenberg

Riverdale, NY
January 2020

Permissions

The following chapters in this volume have been reprinted with the permission of the publications in which they originally appeared:

Chapters 1 (*"To the Wonder"*), 12 (*"All is Lost"*), 19 (*"Blue Jasmine"*), 20 (*"The Wolf of Wall Street"*), 21 (*"Museum Hours"*), and 22 (*"Life Itself"*): *Journal of Religion & Film*

Chapter 25 (*"The Revenant"*): *Wall Street Journal*

Chapters 2 (*"Renoir"*), 3 (*"The End of the Tour"*), 4 (*"Nebraska"*), 5 (*"Boyhood"*), 6 (*"Exodus: Gods and Kings"*), 7 (*"Ex Machina"*), and 8 (*"Adaptation"*): *Public Discourse: Ethics, Law and the Common Good* http://www.thepublicdiscourse.com/

Chapters 13 ("Roger Ebert—In Memorium") and 15 (*"The Great Beauty"*): *Bright Lights Film Journal*

Chapter 14 ("Hollywood, the Oscars, and the Missing Modern Jew): *Haaretz*

Chapters 16 (*"Grand Budapest Hotel"*), 17 (*"The Big Short"*), and 18 (*"La La Land"*): *Kamera.Co.Uk Film Salon*

Chapter 24 (*"Tree of Life"*): *The Jewish Advocate*

Chapter 23 (*"The Great Gatsby"*): *Harvard Divinity Bulletin*

Introduction

Why do we watch movies? If we read in search of more life, as Harold Bloom is fond of saying, then we watch movies, I believe, in search of wonder. We watch movies in search of awe-inspiring visions, transformative experiences, and moments of emotional transcendence and spiritual sublimity. In short, we watch movies for many of the same reasons that we engage in religion: to fill our ordinary evenings and weekends with something of the extraordinary; to connect our isolated, individual selves to something that is greater than ourselves; and because we yearn for something that is ineffable but absolutely indispensable.

This book is guided by the belief that the cinephiliac and spiritual impulses sprout from the same seed. Though they may be watered by different fountains, the desire we have to watch movies, and the need we feel to link our lives to the destiny of a historical faith community, stems from an ever-abiding if unstated sentiment that our basic material lives are not enough, that we need something more—movies and the cinema, spirituality and religion—to add an element to our lives that may not be necessary for our physical survival and yet is something we as human beings have always regarded as absolutely necessary for the survival of our souls: the encounter with wonder.

This book, through an exploration of some of the most intriguing films of the past two decades, illustrates how movies are, have been, and always will be partners with religion in inspiring, conveying, and helping us experience what Abraham Joshua Heschel refers to as "radical amazement": the sense that our material universe and our ordinary lives are filled with more wonders than we can ever imagine, if only we know how to look at our world, and at our own lives, with spiritually—and, I would add, cinematically—trained eyes. Religion and film teach us how to look; they open up new

1

vistas, and make the old ones new again. They illuminate the dark places, and drive away soul-stunting doldrums. They show us how humanity is touched by the heavenly, and how even the humblest human being is worthy of our eternal love and infinite concern. This book subscribes wholeheartedly to Swedish director Ingmar Bergman's belief about the power of film, as articulated in his autobiography *The Magic Lantern* (1987): "No form of art goes beyond ordinary consciousness as film does, straight to our emotions, deep into the twilight room of the soul."

It is my hope that readers of this book will not only gain a greater understanding of how film directors use religious themes and theological motifs to tell their cinematic stories, but will also emerge with an enhanced appreciation for how movies—like religions—help us see the sublime amidst the mundane, fill us with love for our fellow human beings, and inspire us to become better versions of ourselves. I hope you come along with me on this journey through religion and film; I'd love to have you on board. As my rabbis used to say, I'll see you in the beit midrash (study hall). And, as Roger Ebert used to say, I'll see you at the movies. . . .

Chapter One

To the Wonder

"The beginning of wisdom is wonder,"[1] said Socrates, and according to Terrence Malick, the same can be said of film. The idea that wonder is the key to attaining wisdom and appreciating life is the thread that is woven through all of Malick's films. And the principal means of observing this thread is the *sensus divinitatis*—the receptivity to the notion that someone, or something, called God exists, that one can relate to this God in some fashion, and that this divinity provides coherence to the universe and lends wholeness to life. Those lacking this *sensus divinitatis*—those who are, in Isaiah Berlin's phrase, "tone-deaf" when it comes to God and those who cannot tolerate abstract, ponderous films in which dialogue is scarce, may not fully appreciate *To the Wonder*.

Malick's film, coming on the heels of his artistic and religious masterpiece, *The Tree of Life* (2011), is a further illustration of his overriding belief that the world is suffused with a mystery that we cannot understand. Much as the biblical psalms are verbal contemplations of the divine rendered in lyrical form, *To the Wonder* is a visual contemplation of the divine rendered in cinematic form, laced with a multitude of psalmic and biblical resonances. "You got me out of the darkness. You gathered me up from earth. You've brought me back to life," could be mistaken for Psalm 30: "I will exalt you, Lord, for You have drawn me up. . . . You have raised up my soul from the lower world; Lord, you have restored me to life from *she'ol*." And, like *Tree of Life*, it is beautiful in both the religious and artistic sense; knowing how to carefully blend these elements into a luscious mixture is Malick's *métier*.

As *Tree of Life* demonstrated, films are "religious" even when they lack overt depictions or mentions of religion when they attempt to point to a greater majesty in the universe, when they guide viewers toward contemplating the wonder and mystery of life, and when they generally touch upon

3

concerns of meaning. Because of Javier Bardem's Father Quintana, this religious motif in *To the Wonder* is not difficult to espy. Quintana's passionate,
tormented search for God renders him Davidic; just as David prays,
"Lord . . . should You but conceal your face, I would be confounded (Psalm
30:8), and "Why, Lord, do you reject me and hide your face from me?"
(Psalms 88:14), Quintana cries out, "Everywhere you are present, and still I
can't see you. How long will you hide yourself?" His other meditations
contain other biblical allusions; "Shine through us" evokes the Priestly bless-
ing of Numbers 6:26, "May the Lord shed his light upon you." And in his
love and care for the most powerless individuals in society, he is Christ-like;
we observe him visiting the sick, the poor, the imprisoned, and the downtrod-
den, struggling to communicate the message of God's love to those who are
most in need of it. A paragon of saintliness, Quintana is also undergoing a
crisis of faith. Nevertheless, he does not permit his existential doubts to
impede his good works, and serves as a filmic example of the religious hero
whose virtuous actions overcome his theological doubts.

Viewing *To the Wonder* only through the prism of religion would result in
a favorable assessment of the film. However, *To the Wonder* is not only
religious poetry, but it is also a film. While this may seem self-evident, the
apparent neglect of various cinematic elements leave the film denuded, and
leaves its audience deprived of what could have been a truly wondrous spec-
tacle had its cinematic and religious elements cohered. Films like *To the
Wonder* and The *Tree of Life* are the cinematic equivalent of abstract expres-
sionist art, and can only be fully appreciated by a rather attenuated niche
audience—an audience that is not stupefied by questions such as "what is
this love that loves us?" But by casting marquee-name actors like Bardem,
Rachel McAdams and Ben Affleck, *To the Wonder* runs into the very para-
doxical problem David Foster Wallace warned against in his essay "Rhetoric
and the Math Melodrama": some contemporary art is "so abstract and invo-
lute and technically complex" that it can only be appreciated by "people with
extensive educations in the history and theory of these arts"; thus, the attempt
to garner a wider audience for these genres by simplifying, popularizing, and
otherwise diluting its artistic purity will alienate the audience who would
truly appreciate it and yet still fail to sufficiently simplify its content to the
extent that it would be liked by those who would not have fully appreciated it
in its pure form.[2] Perhaps Malick thought he could duplicate his rare *Tree of
Life* achievement, in which he brilliantly fused an artistic, theological, and
commercial movie into a coherent film that attained relatively broad appeal.
But this feat was due to *Tree of Life*'s more linear, limpid storyline, its
bravura performances from Brad Pitt, Jessica Chastain, and Hunter
McCracken, and breathtaking imagery that generated a genuine sense of
wonder. Because all those elements are lacking in *To the Wonder* (the irony
that *Tree of Life* engenders more wonder than *To the Wonder* is lost on no

one), Malick fails to replicate *Tree of Life*'s unique harmonization of the filmic, dramatic, artistic, and religious elements. But, much as Joyce's *Finnegan's Wake* is, according to some critics, a glorious disaster, *To the Wonder* is a consequential *auteur*'s magnificent, glorious failure; every great artist is entitled to at least one.

Malick, as usual, has something profound to say: that the search for love, with all its difficulties, vagaries, ecstasies and betrayals, is the quintessential metaphor for the search for God. While this idea may not be particularly novel for those who read *Song of Songs* allegorically, Malick's greater insight, expressed through the vehicle of Bardem's character, is that what is outwardly a purely religious quest—the search for divine love—is one and the same with the longing for human love. But it is unfortunate that he employs a baffling, frustrating, and (much-noted) self-parodying manner for expressing this idea. Faint outlines of a storyline are sketched, and are adumbrated as the film progresses: a man (Neil, played by Affleck) falls in love with a woman (Maria, played by Olga Kurylenko) in France, and, together with Maria's young daughter, they move to Neil's home-state of Oklahoma. While back in Oklahoma, Neil reconnects with his former inamorata, Jane (Rachel McAdams), and Neil becomes torn between them. Meanwhile, Father Quintana (Bardem) struggles with his faith and his vocation. While Quintana's role is not as cliché as Affleck's Neil, it is still far from original. The concept of clergymen undergoing spiritual crisis was famously mined by Ingmar Bergman, most poignantly in *Winter Light*, in which Gunnar Bjornstrand plays a pastor whose theological uncertainties are reflected in his ministerial difficulties. From Claude Laydu in Robert Bresson's *The Diary of a Country Priest* to Joaquin Phoenix in Philip Kaufman's *Quills*, the tormented priest has been a recurring filmic motif. As a priest suffering a simultaneous spiritual and vocational crisis, Bardem's Father Quintana is most reminiscent of Bjornstrand's Tomas Ericsson. However, the interiorized, complex Father Quintana character is far more compelling than the wooden, simplistic Neil, and is one of *To the Wonder*'s redeeming features.

The Neil-Marina-Jane love-triangle is not only hackneyed but as agonizingly affectless as the Affleck character. And unlike *Tree of Life*'s masterful allegorization of a microcosmic human story with the grand cosmic drama, *To the Wonder* cannot quite relate the love-triangle dilemma to the broader mysteries of life and universe. While *To the Wonder* is somewhat similarly suffused with a bevy of wide-shot long-takes of natural beauty that are certainly wondrous, a few beautifully photographed panoramas a masterpiece does not make. While Malick may have intended *To the Wonder* to be a religious film (in the sense that viewing it could elicit the kind of questions of meaning that are addressed by religion), I doubt that moviegoers exclaiming "thank God!" upon the film's conclusion (as I heard one viewer utter at Lincoln Center's Walter Reade Theater) were the sort of religious sentiments he imagined that *To the Wonder* would evoke. In *Tree of Life*, Malick successfully deployed the abstract and the sublime as a means of stimulating a sense of the *mysterium tremendum* in audiences which were not tone-deaf to such a frequency. Yet, whereas the gnomic qualities of *Tree of Life* contributed to its aura of wonder and majesty, the gnomic qualities of *To the Wonder* detract from its sublimity. Other diversions similarly undermine *To the Wonder*'s aura of spiritual majesty. Olga Kurylenko's ethereal quality is mostly lost in her incessant, distracting twirling. And while the film's dream-like visuals and long stretches of silence can engender a state of reverie, as Roger Ebert noted in his review of the film, Neil's prevarications—into which we're given scant insight—likewise detract from the film's transcendent, contemplative aspects. The *Tree of Life* cast expressed the kind of psychomachic characteristics that the actors in *To the Wonder* do not. Because of this severe want of discernible interiority (save for Bardem's character), *To the Wonder* is severely lacking in the emotive elements that make for compelling cinema.

Joyce did not write another novel after the glorious disaster of *Finnegan's Wake,* dying shortly after its completion. Malick aficionados can take solace in the knowledge that *To the Wonder* will not be his last effort—he has another film currently in production, *The Voyage of Time*—but can only hope that *Voyage of Time* hues closer to *Tree of Life* than *To the Wonder*.

NOTES

1. This quote is commonly attributed to Socrates but its exact genesis is unknown.
2. David Foster Wallace, *Both Flesh and Not: Essays* (New York: Little, Brown and Company, 2012), 215.

Chapter Two

Renoir

The French Impressionist Pierre-Auguste Renoir was not only a prolific creator of gorgeous art, but was a passionate, zealous advocate of creativity itself. The serene, sensitive film *Renoir* (2012) by Gilles Bourdos attempts to match Renoir's lyrical use of color with the lushness of a luxuriously paced film. Much of the out-of-focus, hazy cinematography is designed to mimic the lush, impressionistic look of much of Renoir's paintings. Many shots bathe the screen in the iridescent golden glows of the midday sun. Speckles of light and vibrant colors seep onto the screen in a manner similar to the way they decorate Renoir's paintings.

The film is worth watching not only for its beautiful visual effects, but also for its powerful expression of Renoir's implicit theology of creativity—a theology that has surprising parallels with the thought of influential Jewish thinkers.

At the film's opening, Pierre-Auguste worries that his sons Claude and Jean are not involved in valuable work. "They don't create anything lasting," laments Renoir, "a pair of shoes, a book, a table . . . something people can hold in their hands."

Even before he became a painter, Renoir strove to create objects that could last. As a child, Pierre-Auguste made pottery in a porcelain factory. Creativity was always foremost in his consciousness; it was his *raison d'être.* If his sons were to embark upon paths in which they would not be creative— Pierre was pursuing an acting career and Jean went on to become the famed director of cinematic masterpieces such as *The Rules of the Game* and *The Grand Illusion*—if they did not lead lives in which they created lasting objects that others could "hold in their hands," Renoir feared that they would be wasting their lives.

The loosely structured, nearly inconsequential plot of the film centers on the budding relationship between Jean, who is on medical leave from the French army during the First World War, and Renoir's new model, Andrée. Every artist needs a muse—whether the muses are other works of art (as they were for Yeats), dreams (as they were for Edgar Allan Poe), or God (as He was for the ancient Israelite poets who attributed their wondrous literary creations to divine inspiration). For Renoir, who loved to paint the female nude, his muse was a woman. Or, more precisely, his muses consisted of an alternating cast of younger and younger models; when his models became too old, they were demoted to the Renoir housekeeping staff.

While Renoir was an artist and not a theologian, the theology that is implicit in Renoir's approach to life and to art reflects the centrality of creativity to his thinking. Renoir's theology, it seems, *was* art: just as his lines lent his paintings their form, art endowed his life with structure. And much as his art enriched the lives of others with beauty, art lent his own life a transcendent significance. By creating beautiful objects of lasting value, art allowed him to feel that he was using his artistic gifts in the most beneficial, dignified way possible. To live a meaningful life, for Renoir, was to create.

Renoir possessed a deep-seated belief that existence was rendered meaningful through creativity. Renoir *had* to paint; for Renoir, the stakes of art were almost *yehareg v'al ya'avor*—do or die. If he could not paint, he did not want to live. In the middle of the film, we see him struggling mightily just to walk a few steps. "I give up," he says. He was suffering from cripplingly painful rheumatoid arthritis, and needed to exercise in order to manage his pain. "Walking takes all my strength," he bitterly states, intimating that he wishes to give up the trying regimen. "I won't have anything left for painting."

"And if you can't use your hands?" his assistant asks.

"I'll paint with my dick."

This line may be said for laughs, but it encapsulates an entire realm of thought in which creativity is sexualized, and in which the creative process is viewed as a generative act. If human beings are commanded (or blessed, according to what is perhaps the literal meaning of the verse) to "be fruitful and multiply" (Genesis 1:28), one such manner in which this verse can be fulfilled, according to theopoetic theologians, is to be artistically fruitful and create lasting works of art that fill the world with beauty. "The Renoirs refused to paint the world black," the film tells us. For the Renoirs, the imperative of painting was to make the world beautiful: "There are enough unpleasant things in life. I don't need to create any more."

Creativity as a theology is not confined to artists alone; it is also the theology that animates some of the most influential Jewish thinkers of the past half-century. According to Rabbi Joseph B. Soloveitchik, God created human beings in His image so that they would partner with Him in perfecting

His unfinished world. To be in the image of God, according to Rabbi Solo-veitchik, means to possess some of the capacities of God. Invoking the Tal-mudic concept of *sh'lucho shel adam k'moto* (the idea that one's agent must be like oneself), Rabbi Soloveitchik explains that God was "legally" able to select human beings as His agents because only human beings possess the God-like capacities of the Sender.[1] And foremost among these capacities is the creative capacity.

Being in the image of God, according to Soloveitchik, means that human beings possess a God-like creative capacity. To exercise that capacity is to actualize one's own inner godliness; not to exercise this capacity is to fail to realize one's potential as a creature in the image of God. The "concept of the obligatory nature of the creative gesture—of self-creation as an ethical norm, an exalted value"—was an idea that "Judaism introduced into the world," writes Soloveitchik. The stakes are great, and Renoir appears to have been catalyzed by this notion.

Rabbi Soloveitchik believed that human creative powers were best uti-lized in the service of *chidush*: novel interpretations of text. Renoir believed that human creative powers were best utilized in the service of painting—and if one couldn't paint, then in making shoes, in binding a book, or in crafting a piece of pottery—in creating something that a person could hold in his or her hands, "something that would last."

Soloveitchik, though, also believed that human beings must use their creative capacities on their own selves: "God wills man to be a creator—his first job is to create himself as a complete being." And, as Abraham Joshua Heschel stated toward the end of his life, one should "build a life as if it were a work of art. . . . Start working on this great work called your own exis-tence." As far as Pierre-Auguste was concerned, the process of creating art was the means through which one achieved self-creation.

As the elder Renoir was in painting, so was his son in film: the acclaimed director Jean Renoir created himself by crafting artistic films of enduring cinematic value. Even though he was destined to become one of the greatest directors of early cinema, Jean Renoir himself doubted whether film could ever be "artistic." During the film, we hear Jean expressing profound concern about whether film could ever approach the aesthetic and intellectual plane of painting. "Film is not for us French, it's for the masses," he worries about his chosen field of art. "We have too much artistic baggage." Yet, with triumphs of the celluloid such as *La Règle du jeu,* he would go on to prove himself—and other early cinema skeptics—startlingly wrong.

Jean Renoir and the film *Renoir* alike make the argument that a film, just as much as a painting, can be a lasting work of art. An actor who creates a poignant theatrical performance with his or her voice, body, and gestures, and a director who captures these actions on film, edits them, and shapes them into an aesthetically valuable work of cinema, engage in creative acts as significant as the art of painting. And indeed, just as Pierre-Auguste Renoir's paintings have lasted, Jean Renoir's films have endured the test of time. Both have become works of art that people can "hold in their hands."

"You can't understand painting," said Renoir. "You have to feel it." After viewing *Renoir,* one goes from merely understanding the painter to nearly achieving a sensuous feeling of the great *sui generis* Impressionist himself.

NOTE

1. R. Joseph B. Soloveitchik, "Agency [*Sh'liḥut*]," in *Yemei Zikaron* (Aliner Library; WZO, Dept. of Torah Education & Culture; Jerusalem: Orot, 1986), 9–28.

Chapter Three

The End of the Tour

"It may be what in the old days was called a spiritual crisis or whatever," says David Foster Wallace (as played by Jason Segel) at a key moment in *The End of the Tour*, James Ponsoldt's poignant film about the brilliant late writer. He continues:

> It's just the feeling as though the entire, every axiom of your life turned out to be false, and that there was actually nothing, and it was all a delusion. And that you were better than everyone else because you saw that it was a delusion, yet you were worse because you couldn't function.

Anyone who has ever read David Foster Wallace knows that the man behind the propulsive prose must have had demons upon demons. If reading Virginia Woolf is like eating chocolate and reading Toni Morrison is like drinking wine, reading David Foster Wallace is like taking drugs. One gets an inexplicable high from reading his writing; like an intensely flavorful amphetamine, it keeps readers coming back to his peerless prose again and again.

The man himself, the twentieth-century's literary Mozart behind the bandana, suffered throughout his abbreviated existence from such a severe form of depression that he eventually took his own life at the age of forty-four. The tragedy of his life is that he was never able to escape the very same demons that may have inspired him to create his incomparable brand of extremely addictive writing.

TRAGIC BRILLIANCE

Jason Segel portrays the famed writer with the correct amount of candor and reserve, sprinkling in Wallace's palpable existential anxiety at strategic moments while never losing track of his acutely self-aware way of analyzing every encounter. The premise of the film, which recounts *Rolling Stone* reporter David Lipsky's (Jesse Eisenberg) five-day interview with Wallace at the end of Wallace's 1996 book tour for *Infinite Jest,* seems simple. But with Wallace, nothing was ever simple. Lipsky eventually wrote a bestselling book, *Although Of Course You End Up Becoming Yourself,* based on his interviews with Wallace. In addition to any ironic or existential meaning it holds, the book's title, which is taken from a Wallace quote, turns out to be an apt description of Jesse Eisenberg's performance in this film (and in nearly all of his films), where he usually ends up playing a version of himself.

The real revelation is the excellent screenplay of Donald Margulies. The film has an intimate, theater-like quality to it. It almost seems that the movie might work better as a two-man play; it is thus not surprising to learn that Margulies has written for the stage. The other real surprise is Segel, who depicts Wallace as a man consciously and subconsciously crying out for meaning in his life. Segel portrays Wallace as a man who had experimented with so many ways of living and so felt as if he had exhausted them that by the age of twenty-eight he was already waging an inner war with himself—a war that eventually led him to end his life.

Perhaps the greatest tragedy of Wallace's life is that—for all his brilliance—he could never find a means of filling the dry void in his life with the waters of meaning. According to rabbinic legend, Moses' father-in-law Jethro experimented with every manner of idolatry and religion then available before finding the faith of Moses. Like Jethro, Wallace experimented with an infinite number of ways of life, but he never seemed to find the way that would have saved him from himself.

LONELINESS, SUICIDE, AND RELIGION

Long before the alienation and ennui that afflicted Wallace's Generation X, the acclaimed sociologist Émile Durkheim diagnosed the ills that were plaguing his own generation in the late nineteenth century. Nearly one hundred years before the publication of *Infinite Jest,* Wallace's epic novel about loneliness and alienation, the French-born founder of the modern discipline of sociology produced an epic study of suicide.

In his 1897 work, Durkheim found that suicide rates were higher among Protestants than they were among Catholics and Jews. Durkheim's interpretation of this disparity was startling. In his view, Protestants tended to commit suicide in higher proportions because their faith fostered a greater sense of individualism. This, in turn, led to higher rates of the crippling side effect of loneliness—or, as Durkheim termed it, "anomie" (transmuted into French from the Greek *anomos,* "lawless," and defined as "the lack of social or ethical standards in an individual or group"). Durkheim posited that Catholics and Jews committed suicide less frequently because their faiths placed a greater emphasis on communalism and unity, which engendered among their adherents a sense of togetherness and belonging. Catholicism and Judaism ensconced the individual within a communal web of care and concern, making troubled individuals feel as if they were never truly alone.

Like many sophisticated individuals today, Wallace may have considered himself too intelligent to bother with belief or accept the doctrines of a religious tradition. To many intelligent people, certain core religious beliefs can seem absurd: a divine revelation in the desert that happened before the eyes of three million people? A virgin birth? A resurrection of the Son of God? A resurrection of the dead during the end of days? An all-seeing omniscient being who watches over us and records our every act? These beliefs can seem more fantastic than the most incredible science fiction.

Yet the societies wherein these beliefs emerged created communities of concern in which every individual is cared for and made to belong. In these communities of concern, individuals are given a sense of meaning in life, and are embedded in networks of love and support. As Alain de Botton argued in *Religion for Atheists,* atheists are wrong to reject religion in totality simply because there are certain creeds that they cannot accept. According to de Botton, even atheists should acknowledge that religionists have been geniuses at creating communities and generating meaning; atheists have much to learn from how religion has served humanity's most profound psychological and existential needs for thousands of years. And the secular world has yet to create anomie-reducing alternatives the likes of which religion carefully created and developed over scores of generations.

IS THE UNIVERSE TRAGIC OR COMIC?

At one point during Lipsky's interview, Wallace affirms his belief that human beings cannot truly change. Clearly, Wallace wasn't only a tragic writer. In his real life, Wallace himself was a tragic character who believed that we cannot escape our character, that "in the end we end up becoming ourselves."

This view is fundamentally at odds with the Judeo-Christian tradition, which at its core maintains the hope that we can all change, that we can all purify our coarse characters and merit redemption and salvation. *How* we merit this salvation—whether by accepting Jesus Christ as Lord and Savior or by accepting the yoke of the six-hundred-thirteen commandments—is the subject of doctrinal dispute. Yet what is agreed upon, not only by Christianity and Judaism but by most religions, is that metaphysical, social, and psychological mechanisms exist whereby we mortal human beings can alter the course of our destinies, transcend fate, and achieve—either in this life or the next—inner peace.

Wallace's belief in the futility of human beings' attempts to escape themselves and transcend their natures, and his view that personality is determinative of destiny, suffuses *Infinite Jest* with a tragic sensibility that is closer to the Greek view of human nature than the Judeo-Christian perspective that "every human being has the capacity to be as righteous as Moses or as wicked as Jereboam," as Maimonides wrote in the *Mishneh Torah*. In a key passage of his magisterial *Infinite Jest*, Wallace writes:

> The true opponent, the enfolding boundary, is the player himself. . . . *You compete with your own limits to transcend the self in imagination and execution.* Disappear inside the game: break through limits: transcend: improve: win. . . . You seek to vanquish and transcend the limited self whose limits make the game possible in the first place. It is tragic and sad and chaotic and lovely. *All life is the same*, as citizens of the human State: *the animating limits are within*, to be killed and mourned, over and over again. [1]

Perhaps the true tragedy of Wallace's life was that he was never given the tools to access a religious tradition that would have given him the means to treat the spiritual crisis from which he so acutely suffered. He was never given the spiritual keys that would have unlocked for him the treasure house of a wisdom tradition. Thus, he was always trapped inside his own animating limits, killed by his own hand and mourned by us all.

NOTE

1. David Foster Wallace, *Infinite Jest* (New York, Little, Brown and Company, 1996), 84. (emphasis added)

Chapter Four

Driving to *Nebraska*

Cinema, Human Dignity, and the Elderly

At times, cinema succeeds where philosophy fails. Films like *Nebraska* show us the importance of honoring our elderly parents and remind us of the unique dignity of every human person.

Is it possible for a film that was nominated for six Oscars, was directed by one of Hollywood's most highly regarded filmmakers, and features a career-best performance by one of the best actors of his generation to be over-looked? In the case of *Nebraska* (2013), the answer is yes.

Directed by Alexander Payne and featuring stalwart character actor Bruce Dern in a performance that garnered him his first-ever Academy Award nomination for Best Performance by a Leading Actor, *Nebraska* was one of the surprise standouts of last year's crop of Oscar-season films. The movie is shot in crisp black-and-white, simultaneously conveying the grimness of the forlorn Midwest landscape and also lending the film, in the words of its director, an "iconic, archetypal look." A quiet and subdued film, *Nebraska* imparts an important reminder of every person's intrinsic human dignity, honestly portraying one man's struggle to care for his aging parents in a way that reflects that dignity.

AN AMERICAN ROAD TRIP

In *Nebraska,* Woody Grant (Bruce Dern) is a retired Montana mechanic and a cantankerous Korean War veteran. As if his congenital crabbiness were not enough, Woody is also an alcoholic, and he's evidently verging on dementia. When he receives a promotional sweepstakes letter in the mail stating that he has won a million-dollar prize, he believes it. Everyone understands that this sweepstakes letter is clearly a hoax—everyone, that is, but Woody. He prevails upon his son David, played by a surprisingly effective and restrained Will Forte (formerly of *Saturday Night Live*), to drive him to Lincoln, Nebraska—where the sweepstake's headquarters are located—in order to collect the chimerical prize. They are accompanied by Woody's wife, Kate, played by a wonderful, laceratingly witty, acidly funny, scene-stealing June Squibb who, at the age of eighty-four, received an eminently deserved first-ever Oscar nomination for her supporting actress performance.

As the story unfolds, *Nebraska* seems to follow the structure of the venerable American "road-trip movie." Characters embark on a physical journey across the broad, expansive landscape of our beautiful country, experience interesting adventures, encounter strange and exciting people, and narrowly escape from a few hairy situations, only to experience a more profound inner journey of the soul. Of course, such narrative structures have an impressive pedigree that precedes American culture: think of Homer's *Odyssey,* Swift's *Gulliver's Travels*, or even Dante's *Divine Comedy*.

Yet *Nebraska* is much more substantial than the average American road-trip movie. While our expectations of witnessing the typical tropes of the road-trip genre are fulfilled, the Grants' journey through the lonely land at the center of our country serves as an unconventional exploration of the challenges of honoring our parents. Throughout the film, the message is clear: the elderly—even when they reach the stage of senility—must be cared for with sensitivity and respect.

In choosing to drive him from Billings to Lincoln, David succeeds in pulling off the tricky task of managing a mentally ailing parent. David addresses the dilemma of how he should honor his father by deciding to play along with his father's delusions, in order to avoid causing him needless emotional anguish. David intuitively realizes that more harm would be done by refusing to take his father to Nebraska than by actually making the trip from Montana. Often, when a loved one suffers from early onset dementia, all that their caregivers can do for them is play along. Refusing to do so only makes things worse. Although David's choice compromises on truth, it brings his father emotional peace and preserves his dignity.

Woody, a retired mechanic, intimates that he's merely a beat-up car. But David doesn't buy into his father's mechanic-mentality—he doesn't treat his father as an old machine that is breaking down. Rather, he treats his father as a human being: a unique creature that, regardless of his physical or mental condition, always possesses infinite value and therefore always deserves to be treated with utmost dignity.

MAN IS NOT A MACHINE

The insidious "man as machine" metaphor—as Abraham Joshua Heschel wrote in *Who Is Man?*—may have its source in La Mettrie's *L'Homme machine,* and goes back at least as far as Descartes's *Treatise of Man.* It continues to be promulgated by behavioral scientists and evolutionary biologists as well as ethical humanists and philosophers. Yale Professor of Philosophy Shelley Kagan, for instance, argues that we are machines—incredible, beautiful, thinking machines, but nevertheless machines.

We should be very wary of this definition. As Heschel warned,

> We must not take lightly man's pronouncements about himself. They surely reveal as well as affect his basic attitudes. Is it not right to say that we often treat man as if he were made in the likeness of a machine rather than in the likeness of God? [1]

In an industrialized, utilitarian, youth-obsessed, mechanistic, capitalistic society in which human beings are often viewed as important only insofar as they are capable contributors and producers in the market economy, we run a great risk of unconsciously (and at times consciously) devaluing others once they reach old age and infirmity. If a person can no longer contribute to society in a manner that can be quantitatively recognized—in other words, can no longer buy or sell things—what value does this person possess?

It is precisely in its unequivocal answer to this question—its statement that human beings continue to possess infinite value even when they become elderly and infirm—that *Nebraska*'s power lies. The movie gives a subtle yet clear-eyed depiction of what it means to honor the elderly (Leviticus 19:32) and to honor one's parents (Exodus 20:12, Deuteronomy 5:16). It unapologetically depicts the difficulty of this task, but demonstrates that it is indeed possible.

Nebraska's director, Alexander Payne, is remarkable for, among other things, the consistent cinematic concern he has shown for the elderly and incapacitated. *About Schmidt* (2003), another road-trip movie, also centered on a newly retired and recently widowed man (played by a wonderfully subdued Jack Nicholson) from Nebraska who sets out on a journey to find a sense of purpose and meaning in his life. *The Savages* (2007), for which Payne was executive producer, featured Philip Seymour Hoffman and Laura Linney as emotionally distant, artistically inclined siblings who must come together to care for their father in his final days.

In presenting his cinematic answers to the question of who man is, Payne affirms who man is *not.* In marked contrast to those like James Barrat who raise the specter of artificial intelligence as the beginning of the "end of the human era," Payne affirms that we are *not* machines. And although we are biological creatures, neither are we only biological animals, as those like Michael Gazzaniga would claim. Unlike animals, we not only behave, but we reflect upon *how* we behave. As Harold Bloom has observed, we are beings who not only think, but who overhear ourselves thinking and can change after overhearing ourselves.[2] We are human beings, which means that we are significant, that we have inner identities, that our lives our meaningful, and that our existence is needed.

At times, cinema succeeds where our philosophy fails us. Films like *Nebraska* show us, not through casuistic arguments but through facial expressions, camera work, and dialogue, that we are *not* sub-personal animals, and we are *not* glorified machines: we are *sui generis* creatures known as human beings—dependent rational animals, as Alasdair MacIntyre put it.

Woody Grant is not an interchangeable part in the assembly line of the global market economy—and neither are we. We are not *Brave New World*'s hatchery humans who are bred and programmed as identical, non-unique beings who are prepped to be plugged in to the assembly line of a mechanized world. No, we are *b'tselem Elokim:* creatures made not in the likeness of machines, but in the likeness of God. We are unique and irreplaceable, even when we are elderly and are losing our faculties . . . and even when we are bumbling, broken-down auto mechanics who want nothing more than a trip to *Nebraska*.

NOTES

1. Abraham Joshua Heschel, *Who Is Man?* (Stanford, CA: Stanford University Press, 1965), 24.
2. Harold Bloom, *How to Read and Why* (New York: Touchstone, 2000), 79–89, 147, 194.

Chapter Five

Boyhood

A Profoundly Human Story

Richard Linklater's film is powerful because it reminds us that the dull, plotless events of our fleeting lives matter in the way in which all quotidian things matter: as Joycean "epiphanies of the ordinary."

Boyhood is one of the most special movies of this decade, but it is not one of the best movies of this decade. It deservedly received a bevy of Oscar nominations—six in all, including nominations for Best Picture, Best Director, and Best Screenplay, but winning only for Best Supporting Actress (Patricia Arquette).

Why has *Boyhood,* a modest film with a paltry budget of only $4 million (by contrast, *Guardians of the Galaxy* had a budget of $170 million), received so much attention? The first two reasons for the garlands that this good movie has garnered are obvious; the third reason is much less obvious, but much more important.

First, this film has received so much attention not because of the story it tells but because of the story of how the movie was made. It is the only dramatic (non-documentary) movie in cinematic history to have been filmed over a twelve-year span, with the same cast, shot by the same director. *Boyhood*'s story could not be simpler: it charts the growth of a family—and the growth of one young boy in particular—over twelve years. We follow Mason (Ellar Coltrane) from the time he is five years old until he is ready to go off to college at the age of eighteen. In other words, we witness his growth from a child to an adolescent on the verge of adulthood.

Second, this is one of the more "relatable" films of recently memory. There are no superheroes, no special effects, and no strange twists of fortune and fate. Instead, there is a brother, a sister (Lorelei Linklater, the director's daughter), and a mother (Patricia Arquette) and father (Ethan Hawke) who are divorced. There is no real "plot"; rather, there are a series of episodes from the family's life. Everyone who watches this movie will see something strikingly similar to an event, relationship, or emotion one has experienced in one's own life, because this is a movie that could be made about any life. It is a film about one particular family, but it is a film that could be made about any family.

EPIPHANIES OF THE ORDINARY

Though Patricia Arquette and Ethan Hawke have never been better, the boy is, well—how should we put this?—"meh." Let's remember that at five years old, he was not an "actor" who "chose" this project in the way that Ethan Hawke did; his parents volunteered him for the role when he was a child. Fortunately, the quality of the boy's acting is, in a certain sense, inconsequential to the meaning of this movie. In fact, one could argue that the boy's blandness in fact bolsters the film's brilliance; the boy is an archetype, a blank slate upon which we all project the memories of our own childhoods and relive those long-forgotten moments of our earliest years.

There is no "story" per se in *Boyhood,* but the movie houses a profoundly human story at its heart. *Boyhood* illustrates Jewish political philosopher Leo Strauss's astute observation that we must begin with the particular in order to reach the universal, for the universal grows out of the particular. Even though we may reach the universal, we never completely disassociate ourselves from the particular—and it is through particular love (love for our self, for our family, for our tribe, for our country) that we reach universal love for all humankind. Thus, it is precisely because *Boyhood* is a *particular* story, set in a particular town, and taking place in a particular state, that it becomes a universal story in its appeal and in its import.

But the universalism, as Saul Bellow reminds us in his great novel *Herzog,* must cohere into something larger, more significant, more meaningful:

> All children have cheeks and all mothers spittle to wipe them tenderly. These things either matter or they do not matter. It depends upon the universe, what it is. [1]

Boyhood resonates because these things *do* matter. And these things matter because we *do* choose to see ourselves as living in a universe where these things matter. And so, it *does* matter that Mason's mom fights through a series of poor marital choices and a difficult career path in order to secure a somewhat stable upbringing for her children. And it does matter that she does their laundry and cooks for them and cleans for them and organizes graduation parties for them. It does matter that Mason's dad tries his best to stay close to his children, and it does matter that he takes Mason to Houston Astros games and camping trips. It matters that Mason's mom tries to coolly distance herself from her children when she sends them off to college, but it matters more that she cannot fight off her irrepressible motherly emotions and ends up crying when Mason departs for the University of Texas.

All of these things matter in the way all quotidian things matter: as Joycean "epiphanies of the ordinary." And these things matter to every family for the same reason this movie matters to everyone who sees it: because the movie functions within us in a profound, deep, and religious manner.

THE COMPRESSION OF TIME

The third reason this movie is so powerful is the most subtle, but most important reason of them all. Whether or not viewers realize it, the film taps into the most primal, primordial, perennial concerns we all have: the unstoppable march of time and the meaning of life.

Boyhood takes twelve years and compresses them into less than three hours. To see the movie's characters rapidly age before our eyes reminds us of our own mortality, and compels us to ask, as Mason asks his father towards the end of the film, "what's it all about?"

Mason: So what's the point?

Dad: Of what?

Mason: I don't know, any of this. Everything.

Dad: Everything? What's the point? I mean, I sure as shit don't know. Neither does anybody else, okay? We're all just winging it, you know? The good news is you're feeling stuff. And you've got to hold on to that.

The feeling elicited by watching *Boyhood* is similar, though not quite as powerful, as the feeling imparted by the magisterial *Up Series,* a monumental project in documentary film in which director Michael Apted took a group of English schoolchildren and filmed interviews with them every seven years from the time they were seven years old up until the present day. The first of these documentaries was titled *Seven Up* (1964); the most recent documentary in the series was filmed when they were all 56 years old: *56 Up* (2012).

When we watch *Boyhood* or the *Up* series, we sense how quickly time moves, and when we think about the passage of time and the swift, inexorable path along which our lives progress, we inevitably ask, "what's it all about?" If we're here for such a short time, and the time we do have flies by, and is lost forever once it's gone—then what's the point? Why do I exist? Why do *we* exist? Does life have a purpose?

But beyond these questions, what is that funny feeling we feel when watching *Boyhood* or the *Up* series? It is a certainly a sentimental, melancholic feeling, particularly for parents who have experienced the roiling emotions of sending a child off to college. It is a feeling of *mono no aware,* a Japanese term I learned about from Roger Ebert, which means the appreciation for, and heightened awareness of, the ephemera of time. It is also, surprisingly—and significantly—a *religious* feeling.

RELIGIOUS FEELINGS

There is something about observing a compression of time, or experiencing the swift passage of time, that engenders those mysterious sensations that we term "religious" (or "numinous") feelings—those sensations we receive that connect us to something that is greater than ourselves; those awe-some feelings of transcendence that sound the simultaneously melodious and awe-full sonnets of the supernatural and the spiritual within us; and those mystic chords of memory that move us to communion with others in our community who live in other regions of the globe and in other times of history.

This is what little Hans Castorp felt when, in Thomas Mann's *The Magic Mountain,* his grandfather would show him the family christening basin:

> On the back, engraved in a variety of scripts, were the names of its successive owners, seven in number, each with the date when it had passed into his hands. The old man named each one to his grandson, pointing with beringed index finger. There was Hans Castorp's father's name, there was Grandfather's own, there was Great-grandfathers' ("*Urgroßvater*"); then the "great" ("*Ur*") came doubled, tripled, quadrupled, from the old man's mouth, whilst the little lad listened, his head on one side, the eyes full of thought, yet fixed and dreamy too, the childish lips parted, half with awe, half sleepily. That great-great-great-great ("*Ur-Ur-Ur-Ur*")—what a hollow sound it had, how it spoke of the falling away of time, yet how it seemed the expression of a piously cherished link between the present, his own life, and the depth of the past! . . . Religious feeling mingled in his mind with thoughts of death and a sense of history, as he listened to the somber syllable; he received therefrom an ineffable gratification—indeed, it may have been for the sake of hearing the sound that he so often begged to see the christening basin. [2]

The little one looked up at Grandfather's narrow grey head, bending over the basin as it had in the time he described. A familiar feeling pervaded the child: a strange, dreamy, troubling sense: of change in the midst of duration, of time as both flowing and persisting, of recurrence in continuity—these were sensations he had felt before on the like occasion, and both expected and longed for again, whenever the heirloom was displayed.

These, then, are the feelings we feel when we see *Boyhood* and the *Up* series: the "falling away of time," the "piously cherished link between the present, [our] own [lives], and the depth of the past"—these are "religious" feelings, and they are feelings that, somehow simultaneously, we both long for and dread, yet long for again and again. These are the feelings that are behind the remarkable resonance of *Boyhood*.

NOTES

1. Saul Bellow, *Herzog* (New York: Penguin, 1961), 38.
2. Thomas Mann, *The Magic Mountain* (trans. John E. Woods; New York: Knopf, 1995), 21.

Chapter Six

Exodus: Gods & Kings

What Does God's Voice Really Sound Like?

With its controversial decision concerning the Voice of God, the movie *Exodus: Gods & Kings* demonstrates the fact that we cannot state any claims about the nature of God as a matter of fact. We can, however, make truth-claims about what we *believe* to be the nature of God—and within these truth-claims, we should allow for greater, not lesser, diversity of beliefs, for the Bible itself showcases God—and the voice of God—in many different tones.

Ever since Cecil B. DeMille cast Charlton Heston's heavily modified voice as the voice of God in his *Ten Commandments* (1956), we have become so accustomed to thinking that the voice of God is supposed to sound like a deep male voice that the phrase "the voice of God" itself has become a synonym for "deep male voice."

But the voice of God has not always been imagined as having sounded like "the voice of God." The voice of God has at times been imagined as sounding like your parent's voice (which could either be benign, benevolent, or terrifying, depending upon what kind of relationship you've had with your parents); at times, God's voice has been imagined as a "still small voice" (1 Kings 19:12); and at other times, God's voice—when actually heard by the prophet Samuel—was so ordinary-sounding that when God called out to Samuel (1 Samuel 3), Samuel thought it was his teacher Eli. It took God four—*four!*—calls to Samuel to get the young nonplussed prophet's attention that it was actually God on the line, so to speak. (Thus proving that it was God—not Verizon or T-Mobile—who invented Caller ID.)

This is why Ridley Scott's decision to cast an 11-year-old boy (Isaac Andrews, a British actor) as the voice of God in the 3D extravaganza *Exo-*

dus: Gods and Kings, which opened this week, is not only innovative and refreshing, but is in fact restorative and startlingly traditional. The Bible more often portrays God's voice as sounding ordinary and meek (or "still" and "small," as God tells the prophet Elijah what His voice sounds like) than booming and thunderous. The critics who are deriding Scott's decision as heretical, blasphemous, or somehow unfaithful to Scripture, seem to be over-looking Scripture's actual descriptions of God's voice.

To claim that we know anything about God as a matter of factual certain-ty, let alone that we know something as specific as how God's voice sounds, is a fallacy. Theology is not an empirical discipline; we cannot know any-thing of the nature of God in the same way in which we can know the nature of Saturn's rings. The latter, unlike the former, is discoverable through astro-nomic explorations, scientific investigations, and empirical observations. Theology is closer to an art than a science; just as something is "true" in art if it resonates with something deep within us, or is reflective of our emotional intuition of the way in which we experience the world, so too, a theological claim is "true" if it harmonizes with our emotions, is reflective of our lives, or offers us a meaningful narrative for our existence. As the prophet Isaiah—or as biblical scholars would have it, Second Isaiah—himself declared about God,

> To whom can you compare Me
> Or declare me similar?
> To whom can you like Me,
> So that we seem comparable? (Isaiah 46:5)

Even the biblical prophets seemed to understand that, while we could make certain theological truth-claims about God, we could never truly under-stand anything about the nature of God with any degree of factual certainty. We could, perhaps, *experience* [what we believe to be] God's "hand" in history, in our lives, and in whatever we believe to be moments of transcen-dence, but we can never *know,* as a matter of *fact,* what God's "hand" looks like, anymore so that we can ever know if God even has a "hand." [1]

Thus, to claim to know what the voice of God sounds like as a matter of fact is as dubious a truth-claims as a claim that one knows what the exact meaning of Smetana's "Ma Vlast" is with factual certainty. Not only can one not know the meaning of a Smetana symphony with factual certainty, but one cannot even know how exactly the Smetana symphony is supposed to *sound* with factual certainty. Perhaps Smetana intended it to be played in different ways at different times; perhaps Smetana knew that in his time, it would be played one way and later, when the craft of music, the individual members of an orchestra, the variety of conductors' interpretations of the piece—and the instruments themselves—undergoes change, its sound would be subtly but noticeably different. We have evidence—not scientific or historical, but biblical evidence—that, just as God was experienced in different ways at different times in history, so too, the sound of God's voice was experienced in different ways at different times in ancient history.

Moreover, traditional theology—Jewish tradition, at least—insists that God's voice is not uniform: though Jews are monotheists, we do not believe that God speaks in monotone. God's words are polyphonous—subject to multiple interpretations and mani-layered readings. "'Is not my word like fire,' declares the Lord, 'and like a hammer that breaks a rock in pieces'"? says the prophet Jeremiah (23:29). Scripture can encompass multitudes of interpretations (up to seventy, according to Jewish tradition), in part because God Himself is multi-dimensional and cannot be understood in a simple, facile glance. "Truth is various," wrote the prophetic Virginia Woolf in *The Common Reader*; "truth comes to us in different guises; it is not with the intellect alone that we perceive it."[2] According to the talmudic interpretation of Jeremiah—"these *and* these are the words of the living God," for "just as a hammer shatters a rock into many pieces, so does one biblical verse (God's word) convey many meanings"[3]—Ms. Woolf may as well have been writing about theological truth as artistic truth.

And not only is the word of God heard in many different ways, but the voice of God itself, suggests Jewish tradition, is heard in many different tones. When Moses heard God speak to him for the first time at the burning bush, the ancient rabbis stated that God's voice sounded to Moses like that of his father Amram.

If God's image is not exactly in the eye of the beholder—after all, the Bible states that one cannot look at God and live—the sound of God's voice does seem to be in the ear of the listener. According to rabbinic theology, just as Moses experienced God's voice in a certain way, so too, no two individuals experience God in the same fashion; God reveals Himself to individuals in a fashion that "corresponds to the capacity of each individual listener."[4] The Rabbis of the Talmud teach that when God spoke to the entire Jewish people during the theophany at Sinai, each person's understanding of God differed, because God chose to make Himself understood "according to the comprehension of each."[5] The God's-voice-as-Moses'-father theory is the most radical tonal shift of all: it suggests that God, far from being a perfect, solid, never-changing rock, is in fact promethean, mutable, and—yes—even occasionally mercurial. If God's voice changes to suit the ear of the listener, then the divine word—like the sound of the divine voice itself—may also be open to new, multiple tones and interpretations. If, as the rabbis explain, God spoke to Moses with the voice of his father in order to put Moses at ease rather than scare him away with a big, booming Hestonian voice, what's to say that God didn't drop down an octave or two to speak to Joshua with the voice of a young boy? To suggest that God is constrained to only a certain vocal range is to limit the God's power—and what faith-professing Bibliophile would deign to be guilty of such diabolic doubting of the Deity's Do-Re-Me's?

In fact, even though Christian groups have been more outspoken than Jews in their protests against Ridley Scott's use of a young boy's voice as the voice of God, the Christian tradition may contain an even more overt suggestion that the voice of God—or at least voices thought to be associated with the voice of God—*can* be a young child's voice. After all, it was a child's voice that Augustine heard which catalyzed Augustine's conversion process. When Augustine heard a child's voice repeating the phrase "*Tolle, lege*: pick up and read!," he interpreted this voice as a sign from God, opened up the New Testament, and the rest of this mystery is theological history: the most consequential theologian in Western Christianity was born, inspired by a child's voice which he chose to interpret as sent by God.[6]

Yet, even if we are to concede that the divine may deign to speak to individuals with the voice of a child, an even more radical—if still thoroughly traditional—tonal shift is waiting to be made. The Talmud speaks of God as speaking to the wise through a heavenly voice termed a *bat-kol*: literally, a "daughter of a voice." The implication is clear: God can make His—nay, *Her*—voice sound like a woman's voice. If Scott can direct a movie in which a *Gladiator*-like Moses hears God speak to him with the voice of an 11-year-old boy, how far off are we from Kathryn Bigelow's *Book of Judges* movie in which a *Xena: Warrior Princess*-like Deborah hears God speak to her with the voice of an 81-year-old woman? And with a neurotic General Sisera played by Larry David? (Well, this last part may be unnecessary, but "Curb Your Enthusiasm" fans would enjoy the hilariously awkward Larry-Lucy Lawless reunion.) As long as the 81-year-old woman is voiced by a regal-sounding Brit—Judi Dench, let's say?—I'm sure Americans would have no qualms with taking orders from a Heavenly voice that heavenly. (Heck, I wouldn't disobey Judi Dench if she told me to chug a 16-ounce jar of wasabi.)

Would we really be able to stand in fear and awe before a feminine God? If presidential politics are any indication—the early word on the 2016 election is that a certain formidable woman is a shoe-in to become our 45th president—the answer is a resounding yes. I, for one, welcome our new female overlords—er, *Lords,* that should read, at least as far as one of them is concerned—and I would not be afraid if God spoke to me using the voice of a woman. But if He (sorry, old habits die hard) She spoke to me using Meryl Streep's Clarissa Dalloway voice? As a bibliophile, I'd be terrified; but as a cinephile, I'd be delighted: God is just about the only remaining great (female?) historical figure that Ms. Streep has yet to play. Almost a century after Virginia Woolf demanded that women be given a room of their own, perhaps it is well-nigh time that women be given a voice of their own as well. Hollywood, are you listening? Because very, very soon, that authoritative voice in our ears will sound an awful lot more like our mother's than our father's voice. And for this revolutionary night-and-day voyage out of staid scales and modes toward exciting new-wave vocalizations, we have only our uninhibited imaginations—and God Herself—to thank.

NOTES

1. See the work of Maimonides in various places: *The Guide to the Perplexed,* generally, and *Mishneh Torah* [Code of Jewish Law], "Laws of the Fundamentals of Torah," 1:12; cf. ibid., 1:9.

2. Virginia Woolf, "On Not Knowing Greek," in *The Common Reader* (ed. Andrew McNeillie; New York: Harcourt Brace Jovanovich, 1984), 32.

3. Babylonian Talmud, *Sanhedrin* 34a.

4. B.T., *Bava Metzia* 59b.

5. B.T., *Chagigah* 13b.

6. See Augustine, *Confessions* (trans. Henry Chadwick; New York: Oxford University Press, 1991), VIII: xii, p. 29.

Chapter Seven

Ex Machina

"If you've created a conscious machine," says Caleb to Nathan towards the beginning of *Ex Machina* when Caleb discovers that Nathan is on the verge creating an artificial intelligence that is indistinguishable from human intelligence, "it's not the history of man. It's the history of Gods."

Ex Machina, written and directed by Alex Garland, is an intriguing film about the wonders and dangers of artificial intelligence (a.k.a. AI). Garland's tale is stylishly told, beautifully photographed, and aided by a clever script that subverts standard cinematic clichés. It is fascinatingly unpredictable at every turn, right up to the film's final scene. It is also suffused with religious themes and theological motifs. Ever since Mary Shelley's *Frankenstein,* the prospect of human beings creating human-like beings of their own has almost always invariably raised the issue of "playing God."

In *Ex Machina,* Caleb (Domhnall Gleeson), a computer coder brought to Nathan's (Oscar Isaac) secret research facility to apply the Turing Test to Nathan's AI—that is, to test whether a human interacting with the robot would be able to tell that the AI is non-human—compares Nathan to J. Robert Oppenheimer, one of the principal creators of the atomic bomb: "I am become death," Oppenheimer said, referring to the Hindu god Vishnu, "destroyer of worlds." This is precisely what could happen if humanity's experiments with AI go wrong. In building Ava (Alicia Vikander), the first fully "human" robot in both appearance and intelligence, Nathan also compares what he has done to Prometheus, the mythological Greek deity who stole fire from the gods. This comparison may be the film's central supporting beam upon which the rest of its story—and its literary, cinematic, and theological allusions—are placed. In creating a new form of human-like life, Nathan is a futuristic Victor Frankenstein; both "stole" (learned how to create) "fire" (the secret of life) from "the gods" (science); hence, Nathan's comparison is as apt as Mary Shelley's subtitle for her 1818 masterpiece: *"The Modern Prometheus."*

CAN *IMAGO DEI* APPLY TO ARTIFICIAL INTELLIGENCE?

Linking the film to *Frankenstein* allows the film to not only establish its link to the literary genre of AI-science fiction, but to the religious tradition of creation stories as well. Shelley herself did this by choosing a passage from John Milton's *Paradise Lost* (the most important work of theological literature in the English language) for *Frankenstein*'s epigraph. Shelley, like Garland—and like the main characters in the film itself—knew exactly what was at stake when the proposition of humans building other human-like beings is contemplated: nothing less than our understanding of what constitutes a "human being" and, concomitantly—or consequently—our conception of God.

If to be human is to be a being created in the image of God—to be, as Milton put it in *Paradise Lost,* the "human face divine"[1]—for, in traditional monotheistic thought, it is *God* that has created *us*, then what theologo-anthropological status are we to ascribe to a robot created by us human beings that is for all intents and purposes indistinguishable from us human beings? If we are not prepared to call such creatures "human," then what shall we call them? "Artificially intelligent humans"? Can such creatures be said to be created "in the image of God"? And if so, what kind of God would we be talking about? Why would God give us the scientific ability to create versions of ourselves? How would we reconceptualize our relationship with such a God? What description are we prepared to apply to the creator of such an AI? What will it mean for us, theologically, ethically, and anthropologically, if future man begins to subsume some of God's creative capacities?

RAISING QUESTIONS IN A SCIENCE-FICTION FILM TRADITION

All of these crucial theological issues are implicitly (and occasionally explicitly) raised in *Ex Machina,* the best science fiction film since *Moon* (2009), another excellent film which touches upon some of these issues as well. *Ex Machina,* a film squarely in the Kubrickian "intelligent sci-fi" tradition, raises these issues in a smooth, stylish manner reminiscent of *Gattaca* (1997) in its sleek, sterile futuristic sets, and the Russian sci-fi classic *Solaris* (1972) in its slightly claustrophobic feel. Other films have examined the very likely eventual relationship between humans and AI: notably *Blade Runner* (1982), as my friend Tamir reminded me; Sofia Coppola's *Her* (2013), in which Scarlett Johansson is the voice of a more advanced version of Siri; and, of course, Steven Spielberg's *A.I. Artificial Intelligence* (2001), which was a long-simmering project of Stanley Kubrick's that Spielberg assumed after Kubrick's death in 1999 (the film is dedicated to Kubrick). *Ex Machina,* like Kubrick's *2001: A Space Odyssey,* also takes place in a secluded, sterile environment, employs the barest minimum of a cast, addresses the frightening prospect that future AI may have our intelligence but may not share our moral and ethical values, and, like *2001,* strives to transcend cinema and attempts to succeed on the level of mythology.

2001 was screened at the Vatican, where it received a pleasant reception because it engendered theologically-tinged feelings by causing viewers to contemplate the wondrous beauty and awesome mysteriousness of the universe, God's creation. It may take hell to freeze over for *Ex Machina* to be screened at the Vatican (the viewer will understand), but, in contrast to *2001,* wherein the story of human history was placed within the narrative frame of evolution, *Ex Machina* places the story of our eventual creation of human-like AI within the narrative frame of the Book of Genesis.

(*Spoiler Alert*) Like the biblical God, Nathan creates his humans in a lush, secluded, Edenic enclave of natural beauty. Like God, Nathan *builds* his woman AI; in describing the creation of the first woman, Genesis 2:22 specifically uses the language "build." (Many English bibles follow the imprecise translation of the KJV, translating "*vayiven*" as "made," but the Hebrew *vayiven* really means "and He *built.*"[2]) The most glaring reference to Genesis is the name Ethan bestows upon his first fully "human" AI: "Ava," a name which cannot but conjure "Eve." Moreover, in the Jewish homiletic tradition of the creation story, wherein God has to build 974 worlds—and destroys each one—before finally creating the first genuinely livable world, so too, Nathan, in the film's most horrifying revelation, builds and destroys several earlier, imperfect AI before he finally accomplishes the creation of Ava. As in Genesis (and as in Mary Shelley's *Frankenstein*), Nathan's creation begins to resent him, and eventually commits a rebellious act that results in her expulsion from Nathan's Eden—an expulsion which occurs during Ava's seventh session of testing. (Not uncoincidentally, in the Genesis creation narrative, Adam and Eve's expulsion also occurs on the seventh day of creation.) How Garland portrays Ava's expulsion, though, is radically different from the Genesis tale.

JEWISH TRADITION OFFERS A RESPONSE TO THESE SCENARIOS

The possibility of human-like AI is no longer an unrealistic science fiction fantasy; it is a very real prospect of which we are on the verge of seeing, many of us in our lifetimes. We have already developed "soft AI"—namely,

AI which can process data and information better and more quickly than humans—such a the Watson computer which beat human contestants in *Jeopardy!,* the AI which has consistently beaten chess champions in chess, and the iPhone's Siri, which can understand human questions and respond appropriately. But science experts predict that in as soon as thirty years, we will have "hard AI"—AI which can *think* like human beings, such as the HAL 9000 computer of *2001,* or the computerized voice of Scarlet Johansson in *Her.* Which means that very soon, the classic scenarios of science fiction from *Frankenstein* to *2001* and now to *Ex Machina* will become science fact. And the moral and ethical concerns that such "hard AI" will raise will have to be adequately addressed. I do not propose here to answer any of the multitudinous dilemmas that hard AI will present. I merely propose that it is important that we recognize these dilemmas so that we can begin to address them in advance. And in addressing these ethical quandaries, one helpful way of thinking about the problematics of technology comes from the Jewish tradition.

In Greek mythology, Prometheus is punished by the gods for this theft of fire. But in Jewish mythology, not only is man not punished by God for creating fire, but, as Abraham Joshua Heschel has observed, it is *God* who gave fire to *man.* According to Jewish legend, after Adam's expulsion from Eden, God showed Adam how to create fire by rubbing two sticks together.

From a Greek perspective—the perspective of Prometheus, *Frankenstein,* and *Ex Machina*—the development of new technology is fraught with peril, and can lead to a kind of fall. From a Jewish perspective—and perhaps from a Christian and Western perspective as well—the development of new technology is an inherently positive phenomenon. There are hazards to be had for sure, but what is crucial is that we human beings interact with technology through sacrosanct moral paradigms. It is only when we misuse technology that technology brings evil.

Thus, as with fire, so will be the case with AI—whether it will be good or evil will depend on how we use it. As the *midrash* (Jewish ethical teaching) states:

> When God made man, He showed him the panoply of creation and said to him: "See all my works, how beautiful they are. All I have made, I have made for you. Take care, therefore, that you do not destroy my world, for if you do, there will be no one left to mend what you have destroyed."[3]

Very soon, the classic scenarios of artificial intelligence from science fiction will become reality. Recognizing the moral and ethical concerns such achievements will raise can help us begin to address them. Whether the development of new technology will be good or bad will depend on how we use it.

NOTES

1. Milton, *Paradise Lost* (New York: Barnes & Noble Classics, 2004), III: 44, p. 40.

2. In *Ex Machina*, the creation of the new Eve happens architecturally, she is "built," as the original Eve was "built" ("*vayiven*"). And in the Torah, it wasn't so much that Eve was built out of Adam's "rib," but that she was built out of his *entire side*. In fact, the translation of "*tzela*" as "rib" is one of the worst mistranslations in the history of biblical translation, not just for semantic reasons, but because it is a mistranslation that perpetuated an historic injustice that has only recently, within the past sixty or so years, begun to be reversed.

The Bible Scholar John Walton, in *The Lost World of Adam and Eve: Genesis 2–3 and the Human Origins Debate,* explains that if you look at how the world "*tzela*" is used in the rest of the Bible, it is *not* used anatomically, it is used *architecturally*; thus, *tzela* cannot mean *rib*, but must mean something closer to *side*. The implication being that God did not build Eve out of Adam's rib, but out of Adam's entire *side*, as the Talmud itself states: that originally, Man and Woman were one creature in one body (Babylonian Talmud, *Eruvin* 18a), and thus, when God created—or built—Eve, He built Eve out of Adam's entire other *side*. When God put Adam to sleep and "constructed" Eve, He did not just remove one rib-bone, He removed Adam's entire other *side*. He split Adam in *half.*

The implication is clear: women are *not* men's "ribs," they are men's other *halves*—that is, they are equal in every intellectual, emotional, and spiritual way to men. In part because of this mistranslation, for millennia women were considered unequal to men—a misinterpretation based upon a mistranslation that even John Milton himself notoriously accepted and propounded. If God considers women only the equivalent of a *rib* of a man, then how could women be equal to men? But if women are men's other *halves*—and vice-versa—then of course they are equal to men.

3. Kohelet Rabbah 7:13.

Chapter Eight

How to Overcome the War Within

Lessons from Adaptation,
Oscar Wilde, and the Sages of the Talmud

Modern films, Victorian literature, and Jewish sages illustrate a religiously grounded, morally mature approach to the classic internal conflict identified by great thinkers from Plato to Freud.

"Until how long will you be jumping back and forth between the two sides?" Elijah berates the Israelites who waver between monotheism and idolatry in I Kings 18:21. "Serve God or Baal!"

The classical identity conflict, as described by the Bible, is between "God and Baal." On one side is the proper, pure, Godly side of ourselves that seeks to preserve decorum and always seeks to do the right thing. This is our Apollonian side, our inner Dr. Jekyll. In Freudian terms, this is the superego, or—as the rabbis of antiquity put it—our "Yetser HaTov" ("Good Inclination"). This side is at war with the wild, libertine, devilish side of ourselves that seeks licentiousness and lascivious pleasures: our Dionysian side, our inner Mr. Hyde. In Freudian terms, this is the id; for the rabbis, it is our "Yetser HaRa" ("Evil Inclination"). "The flesh lusts against the spirit," says Galatians 5:17, "and the spirit against the flesh." Plato posited a conflict between our bodies and our souls—he believed that human beings have divine souls but "titanic" bodies (made from the ashes of the burning Titan corpses and out of blood of the Titans shed in their war against the Olympians). Shakespeare, too, often wrote of this inner conflict; in several of his plays, such as *A Midsummer Night's Dream,* lovers flee to The Forest (which represents passion, unbounded liberty, and imagination) in order to escape the unfeeling restrictions of The City (which represents reason, order, and the rule of law).

This innate identity conflict plagues us all. It has been diagnosed by doctors of the soul from Plato to Freud, whose conception of the conflict between the id and the superego—and the attempts of the ego to mediate between them—roughly corresponds to Plato's tripartite theory of the soul, wherein the appetitive soul contends with the rational soul. Likewise, it has been identified and described by great theologians (Augustine), writers (Shakespeare, Dostoevsky, Robert Louis Stevenson), and films (*Fight Club*) across the centuries.

We all have identity conflicts. Some of us are torn apart by indecision, riven between the cautious side of ourselves, which craves comfort and familiarity, and the daring side of ourselves, which seeks adventure and excitement. Should we stick to the same unfulfilling but financially secure job we've had for years, or should we quit and embark on a risky but exhilarating career change? Should we keep dating the same partner, or should we break things off and try to find someone who understands us better? Some toggle back and forth between religiosity and impiety. And others, like Saint Augustine, "vacillate between dangerous pleasure and healthful exercise."[1]

THE LESSONS OF *ADAPTATION*

One of the greatest movies of the past twenty years, Spike Jonze's *Adaptation*, offers an excellent modern exploration of the classic problem of the divided self. Real-life screenwriter Charlie Kaufman of *Being John Malkovich* fame (played by a brilliant Nicolas Cage) is struggling to adapt New Yorker writer Susan Orlean's (Meryl Streep) book *The Orchid Thief* into a screenplay. Charlie treats screenwriting as an art, and agonizes over his artistic choices like a twenty-first-century Flaubert, forever seeking *le mot juste.* His fictional twin brother, Donald—also played by Cage—is a hack screenwriter who views the craft as a business, spouting off film-industry words like, well, "industry," to the eternal exasperation of Charlie. What eats at Charlie even more is that he realizes he needs his suddenly successful dilettante brother's help in order to adapt Orlean's seemingly unadaptable book into a screenplay.

Adaptation is a film about doubles. It takes a second viewing to realize just how important the motif of the double in *Adaptation* is—pun intended, of course, because almost everything in *Adaptation* exists in a second, mirrored, double realm. Even in Donald's hackwork of a screenplay, "the Three," his image-motif of choice is the mirror, and the threadbare story hinges on a madman with a split personality.

Donald, who does not exist in real life but is a persona created by Kaufman in order to dramatize his very real inner conflict, is obviously Charlie's double. But perhaps less obviously, John Laroche (Chris Cooper) is Susan

Orlean's double. Charlie and Susan are respectable, rational writers. They are quiet, sedate, and non-adventurous by nature. Donald and John represent the ids—the Hydes, the Yetser HaRas, the appetitive sides—of Charlie and Susan. Donald and John are unencumbered by conscience and uninhibited by fear. They take the sorts of wild risks with their crafts that Charlie and Susan would never dare. As Susan says about John, he has the kind of passion for something she wishes she could have for anything. As a bee is attracted to the flower it is programmed by nature to pollinate, she is attracted to the side of herself that contains her untapped potential for passionate commitment; she is at first a bit resistant to this side of herself, calling John a creature with "delusions of grandeur." But she slowly comes around to see that this other side of herself contains something she must have, at any cost, for reasons that she may or may not understand.

Similarly, Charlie is at first almost repulsed by Donald's crassness. Yet he slowly comes to realize that Donald's easy-going, adventurous nature has charms of its own—charms that, at some level, Charlie wishes he had. After a zany, ironically deus ex machina plot twist entangles all four characters in a madcap chase scene in a Florida swamp, Donald dies besides Charlie, and John dies in the arms of Susan. The Hydes are killed off—the Baal is defeated by the Godly side as the rational, Apollonian soul triumphs over the appetitive, Dionysian soul—and the Jekylls survive.

GO DOWN INTO THE DEPTHS

The machinations that enmesh these four characters together are inconsequential. The zigzagging intrigues of the story about the orchids and the frenzied chase at the movie's climax serve to illustrate the twists and turns occurring within the conflict-ridden consciousness of Charlie Kaufman's—and our—minds. And what is it that Kaufman's universalized consciousness is trying to tell us?

The message is this: you must choose God over Baal. Your superego, your rational soul—your Yetser HaTov—must defeat your id, your appetitive soul—your Yetser HaRa. But if you want to become a complete, fully actualized person, you must go down into the depths with your id. You must harness the wild, passionate, unbounded parts of your inner double and assimilate them into your own being. By doing so—by imbibing the lifeblood of your inner Dionysus without letting your Dionysus control *you*—you kill your double. And you *must* kill your double or risk being killed by *it*. You cannot keep jumping back and forth between God and Baal. You must learn all you can from your inner Dionysus, understand what useful traits it has to offer you, harness its powers of passion for the good, and, by draining your inner Hyde of its positive forces and assimilating them into your rational soul, kill it.

The Jewish sages teach that the Evil Inclination possesses positive character traits that we need in order to survive: the Evil Inclination is called "very good" (*tov me'od*), because "were it not for the Evil Inclination, man would not build a house, marry a woman, reproduce, or pursue commerce."[2] Similarly, the early Christian theologian Origen of Alexandria (an "Orthodox Gnostic" whose teachings later became very influential in Eastern Orthodoxy) claimed that evil has a hidden good buried within it: even Satan will eventually repent. Our "Satanic," Dionysian ids are our doubles who have to be defeated—but not ignored. We must learn from them, take what we can from them without being corrupted by them, and use their powers for the good.

THE WARNING OF *DORIAN GRAY*

Oscar Wilde's only novel, *The Picture of Dorian Gray,* illustrates in lurid, macabre fashion what happens when the reverse happens. In Wilde's wonderful, surprisingly moral tale (surprising because it was written by an author who famously proclaimed that art should *not* be moral), the eponymous protagonist makes an implicit deal with the devil in order to preserve his beautiful, Adonis-like youthful countenance. But while Dorian ceases to age, his portrait—painted by his fawning admirer, Basil Hallward—does.

Dorian gives in to the wiles of his id and proceeds to live a life of debauchery, shielded against remembrances of his mortality by his perpetually perfect physique. But his conscience, in the form of his portrait—which, in the novel, functions as his double, his superego—begins to haunt him, much as Raskolnikov's consciousness does in Dostoevsky's *Crime and Punishment* and as the narrator's consciousness does in Edgar Allan Poe's *The Tell-Tale Heart.* Every time Dorian commits an immoral deed, his picture becomes uglier. Like the Jewish mystics who could tell what sins people committed by examining their faces, Dorian's sin are reflected in his portrait.

When Dorian can no longer stand the silent rebukes of his portrait—his rational, moral self—he takes a knife and slashes his portrait. But instead of causing his portrait's demise, Dorian causes his own. *Dorian,* and not his portrait, is the one who dies, because while attempting to kill his double, Dorian killed his Apollonian side, his rational soul—his Yetser HaTov. He thought he was killing his Dionysian side, his Yetser HaRa—his appetitive soul—but he in fact killed his Jekyll, not his Hyde. And when you kill your Jekyll instead of your Hyde, *you,* and not your double, are the one who dies.

OVERCOMING THE DIVIDED SELF

Your true self is your Yetser HaTov, not your Yetser HaRa. As the sages of the Talmud put it, we all have an inner voice that proclaims to God, "it is our will to perform Your will, but the yeast in the dough [the Evil Inclination] is holding us back."[3] This is why, in Robert Louis Stevenson's *The Strange Case of Dr. Jekyll and Mr. Hyde,* Jekyll slowly dies after Hyde takes over Jekyll's body. When you let your double—your Hyde, your id, your Yetser HaRa—subsume *you* and kill *you* instead of harnessing *it* and killing *it,* you are the one who dies. This is what happens to Dorian Gray and to the unfortunate Dr. Jekyll. But it is not what happens to Charlie Kaufman and Susan Orlean.

We would all do well to remember the lesson of *Adaptation*—that in order to adapt, we must harness the Dionysian part of ourselves in a positive way. We must discover the good that our evil sides have to offer us. After we do so, we must kill that part of ourselves. But it is only by first assimilating our evil sides' hidden powers of good that we become our whole, unitary selves.

The Jewish sages teach that in the end of days, God will finally bring peace not only to the outer, war-torn world but to the inner worlds of our split-selves. He will kill all of our doubles—He will slaughter the Yetser HaRa (the Evil Inclination) and make a feast out of it for the righteous. When the righteous will see the slaughtered Yetser HaRa, they will cry, because it will appear to them like an unscalable mountain, and they will wonder how they ever managed to overcome it. The wicked will also cry—but they will cry because it will appear to them like a tiny thread of hair, and they will agonize over why they were never able to quash it.[4]

Each of us can choose to go the way of Dorian Gray and Mr. Hyde, or the way of Charlie Kaufman and Susan Orlean. As Maimonides teaches, "each of us has the ability to become as righteous as Moses, or as wicked as Jeroboam."[5] The power to harness our doubles is in our hands; it is the easiest and the most difficult thing to do all at once. But when we finally succeed, we will at last create unity within our fractured selves and bring peace to our divided beings.

NOTES

1. Augustine, *Confessions* (trans. Henry Chadwick; New York: Oxford University Press, 1991), 31.

2. Genesis Rabbah 9:7, Vilna edition; my translation (all translations from Hebrew are mine unless otherwise noted).

3. Babylonian Talmud, *Berachot* 17a.

4. Babylonian Talmud, *Sukkah* 52a.

5. Maimonides, *Mishneh Torah,* "Laws of Repentance," 5:2.

Chapter Nine

Moral Gravity and Spiritual Audacity

The Ethic of "Choosing Life" in Abraham's
Binding of Isaac and Alfonso Cuarón's Gravity

"DO WHAT IS RIGHT," Rabbi Weiss always taught us, "not what is popular." Rabbi Avi Weiss has lived by this principle of azut dik'dusha [spiritual audacity]. And he continues to act as an anchoring force of moral gravity. Rabbi Weiss's moral compass constantly directs us toward Judaism's central religious and ethical ideal: uvaharta bahayim, "choose life."

Rabbi Weiss's 5775 (2014) Shabbat Shuva drashah [address] was entitled "As the World Confronts Terror: Why the Yom Kippur Theme of Choosing Life is More Critical Than Ever." In this drashah, Rabbi Weiss discussed how the story of Akeidat Yitzhak [the binding of Isaac] is not, as certain Christological readings would have it, a story that idealizes martyrdom; rather, Akedat Yitzhak is a story that exemplifies the meaning of Deuteronomy 30:19's teaching to choose life. The binding of Isaac episode, Rabbi Weiss stated, is not about dying for God; the binding of Isaac episode teaches us what it means to live for God.

How do we know this? How can we be so sure of the seemingly counterintuitive notion that the Akeidat Yitzhak story teaches us what it means to choose life? Rabbi Weiss illustrated this hiddush [novel explanation] through a rabbinic teaching in Midrash Tanhuma. The midrash attempts to fill in some of the missing elements in the story of Akedat Yitzhak, an episode whose narrative is enshrouded in a penumbra of ambiguity and whose laconic dialogue wraps a veil of vagueness upon its characters. The Tanhuma attempts to pierce the veil of Abraham's unstated motives and unexpressed apprehensions by presenting us with an occurrence that Abraham may have experienced on the way to Mount Moriah:

> While Abraham and Isaac were traveling on the road to Mount Moriah, Satan
> appeared to Abraham in the guise of an old man and asked him where he was
> going. Abraham answered, "to pray." The old man asked, "Why then are you
> carrying wood, fire, and a knife?" Abraham answered, "We may spend a day
> or two there, and we will kill an animal, cook and eat it."
>
> "Old man," said Satan, "are you out of your mind? You are going to slay a
> son given to you at the age of one hundred! And tomorrow, when you do, He
> will tell you that you are a murderer, guilty of shedding your son's blood."
> Abraham said, "Still, I would obey Him." And Abraham turned away from
> Satan. [1]

I was not present when Rabbi Weiss delivered this drashah [talk] at the
Hebrew Institute of Riverdale on September 27, 2014 (I was home—which is
in western Massachusetts—during that Rosh Hashanah and the subsequent
Shabbat), but I was present when Rabbi Weiss delivered an abridged version
of this drashah at Yeshivat Chovevei Torah Rabbinical School (YCT) on
September 29, 2014 to a full Beit Midrash at YCT. When Rabbi Weiss read
the line, "and then the man said to Abraham, 'zaken [old man]! Why are you
suddenly willing to throw away the son that God has promised you, the son
of your 100th year?!,'" he looked up from the podium, glanced to his left,
and made eye contact with me. "Danny," he asked, "why is this 'old man'
calling Abraham a zaken [old man]?" Somewhat surprised that Rabbi Weiss
would cold-call me and put me on the spot—and knowing that he must be
asking me, and not another Daniel (even though there were five other Daniels
at Chovevei at that time), because he was looking at me (and because he was
calling me "Danny," even though only two or three other people in the world
actually call me "Danny"), all I could muster up was, "Well . . . Avraham
was pretty old, too."

"True," said Rabbi Weiss. "But why was this zaken calling Avraham a
zaken?"

Rabbi Weiss paused. "The zaken who was calling Avraham a zaken,"
explained Rabbi Weiss, "was none other than Avraham himself." This "zak-
en" that Avraham encountered along the road, Rabbi Weiss explained, was
not a real, living, breathing being; rather, this zaken was Avraham's own
consciousness. Avraham was speaking to himself. And throughout his three-
day journey to Mount Moriah, Avraham was wrestling with himself. He was
asking himself, "can it be . . . can it really be . . . that God is asking me to do
this? To kill my son? To kill a human being? To kill the son, the human
being, that God promised me? Can I put an innocent human being to death,
when I know that, more than anything else, the God that I stand for, live for,
and teach others to believe in, is the God of life?"

In a knight's move of midrashic audacity, and biz'khut [in honor of]
Rabbi Avraham Weiss, I offer the following midrash [interpretation] of Al-

fonso Cuarón's 2013 film *Gravity* as an artistic illumination of the meaning of "choosing life" in the context of Avraham Avinu's Akeidat Yitzhak.

"The heavens are the heavens of God, and the earth has been given to human beings."[2] If ever a literal interpretation of this verse from Psalms has been rendered on film, it is presented in Alfonso Cuarón's riveting *Gravity*.

The indefatigable human will to live, even in hostile environments, has been a persistent theme in Cuarón's work. *Pan's Labyrinth* (2006), a film that Cuarón produced, dramatized a young girl's struggle to create an inner life for herself while her adult protectors were trying to survive in Franco's repressive Spain. In *Children of Men* (2006), perhaps Cuarón's best effort until *Gravity*, Theo's (Clive Owen) determination in guiding a pregnant woman to safety in a future dystopian world in which women have become infertile served as a cinematic demonstration of what it means to "choose life" (Deut. 30:19). And in *Gravity*, Cuarón goes one step further by exploring the fierce human drive to live in even the most extreme circumstances: outer space.

"Life in space is impossible." These are the film's opening words, and they are written in white font on the pitch-black background of outer space. This tagline immediately frames the type of space movie *Gravity* will be; it will not be a *2001: A Space Odyssey*, wherein human life in space is as harmonious and peaceful as a Strauss waltz. But neither will it depict space as a place of absolute horror in the vein of *Alien*. Though it is a film very much in dialogue with Kubrick's and Scott's classic films—several shots visually reference *2001*, and the motif of the masculine space-cadet heroine appears to be lifted directly from *Alien*—Cuarón's film is not only visually innovative but thematically groundbreaking as well. Rather than recycling *2001*'s or *Alien*'s conceptions of space, *Gravity* depicts space as the biblical Temple in Jerusalem: a place of both beauty and danger.[3] The sights are spectacular, but the slightest human error or natural impediment can lead to catastrophe. In short, this tagline, and the film in general, is a literal explanation of Psalm 115:16; both *Gravity* and Psalms postulate that human beings are simply meant to exist on planet earth, not in outer space. *Gravity* and Psalm 115:16 both imply that the human effort to conquer the heavens is a foolhardy one that, like the construction of the Tower of Babel, will inevitably result in disaster.

In *Gravity*, however, the disaster that imperils the human effort to conquer the heavens originates from the earth, not from space or from some other heavenly realm. While medical doctor Ryan Stone (Sandra Bullock) and astronaut Matt Kowalski (George Clooney) are conducting routine repairs on the Hubble Space Telescope, the Russians shoot down one of their own satellites. Debris from the shattered satellite is propelled into a violent collision course with Stone and Kowalski's shuttle. When the debris collides with the shuttle, Kowalski and Stone are hurtled away from the destroyed shuttle and compelled to embark upon a frantic mission that necessitates the employment of all of their ingenuity and inner strength in order to save their own lives. How they ultimately do so has been the subject of much debate (astrophysicist Neil deGrasse Tyson has poked holes in the scientific accuracy and physical efficacy of the techniques they employ to reach the International Space Station), but what is significant in *Gravity* is its demonstration of the inner resources human beings possess that propel us to fight for life even in the most desperate of circumstances. If "Judaism and Christianity insist that death must be overcome,"[4] *Gravity* illustrates that the human capacity to overcome death exists even in the harshest regions of outer space.

These regions are displayed in breathtaking splendor by the renowned cinematographer Emmanuel Lubezki, and the moving computer-enhanced photographs of planet earth engender the kind of awe and wonder that the best science fiction films are meant to deliver. The film was originally released in 3D, but the 3D glasses only slightly enhanced the visual pleasure of those already magnificent shots; the three-dimensional photography only truly factored into the viewing experience during the scenes in which space junk seemed to be hurtling directly at us viewers.

The cast of the film, like the space shuttle's crew, is sparse but highly effective. Kowalski is a standard Clooney prototype—suave and überconfident, aware of his powers of attraction upon the opposite sex ("I know I'm devastatingly good looking but you gotta stop staring at me," he deadpans), and endowed with a preternatural degree of sang-froid. As the heard-but-not-seen voice of Houston's mission command, Ed Harris mostly reprises his role as NASA flight director Eugene Kranz in *Apollo 13* (1995) and channels elements of his John Glenn from *The Right Stuff* (1983) in yet another space role; some would add his role as Christof in *The Truman Show* (1998) to this list, though this would be somewhat of a stretch. And in a carefully wrought performance for which she justly garnered an Oscar nomination, Sandra Bullock singlehandedly carries the entire crisp ninety-minute affair. She enables the audience to identify with her extreme anxiety without badgering viewers over the heads with melodramatic hyperventilating—though, in one of the few flaws of an otherwise perfect movie, she does cross this threadbare-thin line at certain points; granted, in what is asked of her in this role, it is a line almost impossible not to cross.

Gravity also suggests that space is like a foxhole: there are no atheists in either place. Or, more precisely, even if there are atheists in space, in certain circumstances, they will still experience a desire to pray. When Stone thinks she's about to die, she wants to pray, but doesn't know how. "No one ever taught me how to pray," she wistfully remarks. In the Russian space shuttle, she sees an icon of Jesus, and in the Chinese shuttle, she sees a figurine of Buddha. Cuarón's camera lingers on these images for a few moments to ensure we don't miss them, as if to say that if Stone is to return to earth, she must believe in something, whether it is Jesus, Buddha, or her own untapped inner strength—if not the transcendent God without, then perhaps the immanent God within.

In fact, that Stone's discovery of her own inner resources occurs in nearby proximity to the close-ups of these religious icons suggests that she may have, in her own way, discovered God. Like Rabbi Irving Greenberg's interpretation of the Torah as narrative, not history,[5] the theologian Rabbi Neil Gillman reads the Bible's account of the revelation at Sinai not as an historically accurate description of an actual event, but as an attempt to put an ineffable, indescribable moment into words.[6] "If the ancient Hebrews did not literally hear God at Sinai as the Bible describes," I asked Rabbi Gillman, "then what exactly was revealed to them? Do you think they invented God?" I asked. A revelation did occur, he responded—something happened in the Sinai desert. But what exactly happened, he said, we do not know, and perhaps never will know. During the Hebrews' journey through the unknown, unforgiving Sinai desert, he explained, they culled all of their collective physical, spiritual, and psychological resources in order to survive. And during this process, they discovered strengths about themselves and unknown inner capacities that they never previously imagined they possessed. This, Rabbi Gillman explained, was their revelation of God. Their discovery of their own inner strength was their discovery of God: "They did not invent God; they discovered God, and invented the metaphors."[7]

In the process of discovering their collective inner strength during the Sinai wilderness, the ancient Hebrews discovered a transcendent God. In the process of accessing inner powers she never imagined she had possessed,[8] Ryan Stone discovers an immanent God in outer space. The metaphor that the Hebrews invented for this discovery of God was the name YHVH (or "Yahweh"); Ryan Stone's invented metaphor for this discovery may be the word "myself." It is this discovery that gives her the further strength to confront her personal Hamletesque quandary:

> I get it, it's nice up here. You could just shut down all the systems, turn down all the lights, just close your eyes and tune out everyone. There's nobody up here that can hurt you. It's safe. What's the point of going on? What's the point of living? . . . It's still a matter of what you do now. If you decide to go then you just gotta get on with it. Sit back, enjoy the ride, you gotta plant both your feet on the ground and start living life. Hey, Ryan, it's time to go home.

How *Gravity* portrays Ryan's manner of addressing her Hamlet dilemma is something that must be seen to be believed—or, perhaps more precisely, it is something that must be believed in order to be seen.

As in *Gravity*, so in the Akeidah: just as Stone's conversation with Clooney, we eventually learn, is really a conversation with herself—Clooney is a personification of her own paralyzed consciousness—the Midrash Tanhuma's zaken [old man] is a personification of Avraham's perambulating consciousness. Just as, after a harrowing ordeal and a near-death experience, Stone eventually chooses life, so too, after a harrowing three-day journey and the near-death of Isaac, Avraham eventually chooses life as well.

I wish to conclude with the following drash. It may be a bit audacious, but if I have learned anything from Rabbi Weiss, it is that if you believe you are right, you most not concern yourself with popularity. And the following drash, I believe—if Rabbi Weiss's interpretation of the Tanhuma is truthful—is, if not right, then true: Avraham passed the test of the Akeidah not because he was willing to kill Isaac, but because, ultimately, he was willing to let Isaac live. When Avraham heard the voice of the angel telling him to desist from killing Isaac, he could have reasoned, "God Himself told me to kill my son, and now an angel is telling me not to kill him? How can I obey the voice of the angel instead of the command of God? In a conflict between the command of the master and the command of the disciple, would one heed the command of the disciple?" But Avraham knew that the angel was correct—Avraham knew that the angel was completely correct to such an extent that the angel's command could even override the command of God. And how did Avraham know this? Because, as the rabbis (and Shakespeare) teach, "this to thine own self be true:" Abraham trusted his own inner moral and ethical intuitions, and stayed true to himself.[9] Avraham knew that God would never, in the end, actually desire him to kill an innocent human being. He knew that the God of life, above all else, desires human beings upon whom He has bestowed the gift of life to continue to choose life.

Indeed, in the ancient world, human sacrifice was not uncommon, and when one believed that the gods had commanded one to sacrifice a human being—even if the human happened to be one's own child—one unequivocally obeyed the command of the gods. When the Greek warrior Agamemnon believed that the gods (Artemis, specifically) demanded that he sacrifice his own daughter (as recounted in Aeschylus's play *Agamemnon*) in order to calm the winds so that the Greek fleet could safely sail to Troy, Agamemnon obeyed without question. This was not considered a "trial" on Agamemnon's part; in the ancient world, sacrificing a child to appease the gods was de rigueur. Likewise, when God commanded Avraham to sacrifice his son Isaac, the "trial" was not whether Avraham would obey God; the trial was whether Avraham would obey the angel—the angel that told Avraham not to heed the original command of God. Avraham passed this trial not when he agreed to sacrifice Isaac, but when he agreed to let Isaac live.

And perhaps, in the spirit of the Tanhuma—and in the audacious, but morally grand spirit of *Gravity* and Rabbi Weiss—even the angel's command to "desist from slaughtering your son" was in fact none other than an emanation from Avraham's own mind. Not only the zaken [old man], but even the angel, was a projection of Avraham's own consciousness. "Desist," Avraham said to himself. "Do not lift your hand upon this lad," the angelic aspect of Avraham's consciousness said. "Yes, you—Abraham, you silly old man you—yes, you may have thought that you have heard the voice of God commanding you to kill your innocent son," said Avraham's angel, said Avraham's inner Gabriel. "But did you really? Did you really hear this voice? Are you sure? Really, really, absolutely, one-hundred-and-fifty percent sure?" said the angelic Voice in his head. "Perhaps God said 'ha'aleihu' (bring him up), not 'shah'teihu' (slaughter him)? And you have 'brought him up,' have you not?" Avraham carefully pondered the words of his inner angels, pored over his soul, checked his ethico-religious moral pulse, and concluded: "No. I cannot do it. I will not do it. I cannot, will not, shall not, kill my son, my beloved son, my innocent son. I may have thought that I heard God tell me to do this, but I cannot believe that this is what I accurately heard, nor can I truly believe that this is what this God truly desires. No—I will not, cannot, shall not do this deed. Ad kahn. Some pagans may venerate Hades, other polytheists worship gods of the underworld, and the Egyptians may have constructed a cult of death, but my God is not like their gods— their gods are gods of death; my God is the God of life. I cannot, will not, shall not kill my son—I shall not do this deed—no. I shall let him live. And I shall pass this teaching on to him, to his children, to his children's children, and to the great nation which God has promised will issue from his offspring: that, more than anything else, the God of life created us human beings in His image so that we may imitate the God of life by creating children, beauty, and wisdom—and by choosing life. And, at the end of his life, when Moses's thoughts could have easily turned to death, this people's great teacher will teach his people the teaching that will become the predominant imperative of their entire civilization: 'choose life, so that you and your children shall live.'"

NOTES

1. *Midrash Tanhuma-Yelammedenu,Va-yera* 22; also found in *b.Sanhedrin* 89b, *Genesis Rabbah* 56:4; *Midrash va-Yosha*; and *Pesikta Rabbati* 40:67–69. Translation from Howard Schwartz, *Tree of Souls: The Mythology of Judaism* (New York: Oxford Univ. Press, 2007), 340.

2. Psalms 115:16; my translation.

3. See Moshe Simon-Shushan, *Stories of the Law: Narrative Discourse and the Construction of Authority in the Mishnah* (New York: Oxford, 2012), 216–19. The Temple was a place of order and purity, but chaos and death could occasionally ensue as a result of human misdeeds and ritual misprisions; God smote Nadab and Abihu for improper behavior in the sanctuary (Leviticus 10:1–7), Uzzah died for touching the Ark whilst attempting to prevent it from falling (II Samuel 6:6–7), and a priest died for attempting to reveal the Ark's location (Mishnah, *Shekalim* 6:1–2); ibid.

4. Irving Greenberg, "On the Road to a New Encounter between Judaism and Christianity," in *For the Sake of Heaven and Earth* (Philadelphia: Jewish Publication Society, 2004), 18. In a

review felicitously titled "Between Heaven and Earth," A.O. Scott unintentionally adumbrated *Gravity*'s Judeo-Christian motif of "choosing life" in noting that the film, for all of its "pictorial grandeur," is ultimately "about the longing to be pulled back down onto the crowded, watery sphere where life is tedious, complicated, sad and possible." A.O. Scott, "Between Earth and Heaven," *New York Times,* 10/3/2013, accessed on December 4, 2013 available at http://www.nytimes.com/2013/10/04/movies/gravity-stars-sandra-bullock-and-george-clooney.html?_r=0&pagewanted=1.

5. Eighth lecture in the course series "Shaping a Religious Response: The Rabbinic Engagement with a World in Transformation," delivered at Yeshivat Chovevei Torah Rabbinical School, December 4, 2013. According to Rabbi Greenberg, the Bible is not meant to be interpreted as a simple collection of facts; rather, it is meant to be read as a narrative, because its selection of specific facts creates a structured story. This story is meant to serve as normative guide for persons attempting to find meaning in life and their place in the world.

6. Neil Gillman, *Sacred Fragments: Recovering Theology for the Modern Jew* (Philadelphia: Jewish Publication Society, 1990).

7. Personal communication. This quote is taken from memory, but I trust that my memory of this quote is accurate; Rabbi Gillman is fond of this observation, and has repeated it in other settings.

8. Spoiler Alert: one of these powers is a keen imaginative capacity. Stone's imaginative capacity allows her to conjure an image of Kowalski. Similar to the rabbinic explanation (*b. Sotah* 36b; *Genesis Rabbah* 86:7; Midrash *Tanhuma* 8-9) of how Joseph was able to resist the advances of Potiphar's wife in Genesis 39:7–23—a "likeness of his father [Jacob] appeared to Joseph" warning him of the consequences of submitting to temptation—a talking, breathing "likeness" of Kowalski provides Stone with the mental fortitude she needs to persevere. Cuarón's use of this filmic device allows this intriguing rabbinic narrative to be understood on a cinematic plane.

9. See Midrash Tanhuma [Vayigash 11] and Avot deRabbi Natan 33:1 on Psalms 15:7, narrating the myth that Avraham's two kidneys taught him Torah—a midrash which poignantly teaches that Avraham's own ethical intuitions—and perhaps ours as well—are religiously significant, and deserve to be heard.

Chapter Ten

Magic in the Moonlight

Does God exist? Does life have any meaning? Does the universe have a purpose? Who among us has not brooded upon these baffling inscrutabilities? Woody Allen certainly has, and his *Magic in the Moonlight* (2014) is his most theological, philosophical, and autobiographical movie yet.

Lord knows Woody Allen has put himself on screen before, but even though he doesn't actually appear in *Magic in the Moonlight*, his presence is so palpable that you could swear he was in it—which, in fact, is this film's one true act of prestidigitation. This is a movie about magic, but Allen's screenplay employs no legerdemain; he reveals his conscience, exposes his deepest existential anxieties, and even bares his soul. Never before has Woody Allen brought forth a film as blatantly autobiographical as *Magic in the Moonlight*. Not that this is a bad thing—John Updike was a notoriously autobiographical writer, usually to great literary effect—it is just that in Allen's latest feature (his forty-fourth, by my count, which doesn't include his made-for-TV movies), the characters sometimes seem more like his mouthpieces than actual cinematic personas.

But oh, what mouthpieces! Where else in modern movies do we hear such monologues? Where else in contemporary cinema can we hear similar disquisitions and deliberations about the existence of God, the meaning of life, and the purpose of the universe? Critics continue to castigate Woody Allen for his alleged cinematic crimes—recycling old ideas, reshuffling used concepts, relying on built-in audience goodwill even though "he has nothing new to say"—but are these really crimes at all? After all, from Monet's water lilies to Cézanne's Mount Sainte-Victoire to Rothko's multiforms, the greatest artists have consistently circled back to familiar themes—but when they do so, they always paint the same scene in a slightly different light, with a slightly different shade of color, and with a slightly but significantly altered perspective.

As in art, so in film: Hitchcock gave us many tremendous tales of mystery and suspense, Tarantino continues to give us superb slugfest spectacles, and Allen continues to give us excellent existential philosophical-comedies, so why do we continue to complain? Is it because of—in contrast to, say, Terrence Malick—the sheer amount of films he has now directed? I suppose we'd also tire of gourmet cuisine if we ate Daniel Boulud's cooking every night for dinner. And if the repetition is the source of our griping, the riposte may come from religion itself: the liturgical masters of the great religious traditions knew that certain messages needed to be repeated day after day, month after month, and year after year in order for people to properly inter- nalize the values that a religious text seeks to convey. For instance, the composers of Jewish liturgy believed that the central Jewish teaching is its monotheistic message; all other Jewish teachings, they knew, would natural- ly flow from an acceptance of the monotheistic creed. Thus, they took a verse from the Torah (Deuteronomy 6:4)—"Hear O Israel, the Lord Our God, the Lord is One"—and placed it in the prayer book. They mandated that it be said once during the morning prayer-service, once during the evening prayer- service, and once again before going to bed, thereby ensuring that Jews would never forget its message of monotheism and the ethical values embed- ded therein. And, by inserting the phrase "Blessed art thou, God, reviver of the dead" into the thrice-daily prayer of the Amidah, they further ensured that the eternal Jewish message of hope—symbolized by the resurrection creed— would never be forgotten as well. The Jewish ecclesiastical authorities surely understood the psychology behind the adage, "the threefold cord is not quickly broken" (Ecclesiastes 4:12).

All of this is not to say that Woody Allen is the second coming of a great Jewish liturgical composer; it is not even to suggest that he's as great of an artist as Monet or Cézanne (notwithstanding Colin Firth's—Allen's *Magic in the Moonlight* mouthpiece—description of himself a great artist). But it is to suggest that the secret of great art, similar to the secret of establishing time- tested religious principles, lies in repetition. We should not be so hasty to dismiss "yet another" Woody Allen film with "yet more armchair philoso- phizing" about the meaning of life.

However—and here is where *Magic in the Moonlight* distinguishes itself from all prior Allen films—*Magic in the Moonlight* is no mere "more arm- chair philosophizing." Yes, Woody Allen has pondered existential issues in many a film past, but never before has he confronted God so openly. Never before has he thought up a film as theologically minded as *Magic in the Moonlight*.

The film's plot may be simple, but its messages are complex. Set in the artistically fertile interwar era of 1920s Europe—a unique historical epoch memorably mined by Bob Fosse in *All That Jazz* (1978)—Stanley Crawford (Colin Firth), a renowned magician whose off-stage specialty is exposing psychics, magicians, and spiritualists as the frauds he knows them to be, is invited to the south of France in order to debunk a spiritualist (Sophie Baker, played by Emma Stone) who has an extremely wealthy American family in her sway. A sober man of science with a cynical disposition, Stanley is naturally skeptical of Sophie's spiritualist "sensations," but the more time he spends with her, the more he is astounded by her seemingly supernatural skills. He eventually becomes so taken with her talents that he starts to the question the very foundations—science, rationalism, and materialism—upon which he has carefully constructed the edifice of his conscience.

Firth's and Stone's chemistry is surprisingly delightful, and their romps recall the great cinematic screwball comedy pairings of yesteryear: Clark Gable and Claudette Colbert in Frank Capra's *It Happened One Night* (1934), and, in particular, Cary Grant and Katherine Hepburn in Howard Hawks' *Bringing Up Baby* (1938), another film featuring a sober man of science whose seriousness is mellowed by a magical woman.

One film, though, stands out as the motivic predecessor of *Magic in the Moonlight*: Adrian Lyne's *Lolita* (1997). Like Lyne's controversial adaptation of Nabokov's controversial novel, *Magic in the Moonlight* also showcases the disconcertingly seedy specter of an older, rational, cynical, intellectual European man becoming infatuated with a younger, wide-eyed, precocious, redheaded American girl. When Stanley and Sophie first form an emotional bond during a road-trip to Provence, we recall that in *Lolita*, Nabokov also used the motif of the road-trip to famous (or infamous) literary effect. And when Sophie cuddles up close to Stanley during one unsettling scene, we notice that Stanley looks like, is dressed like, and even sounds like Jeremy Irons' Humbert Humbert. Sophie is even photographed in the same voyeuristic, "male gaze" manner in which Dominique Swain was photographed in *Lolita*. Is Mr. Allen, who famously said that "the heart wants what it wants," trying to tell us something about the nature of (older) male love? Is there something to be made out of the eerie phonetic similarities between "Stanley" and "Woody," "Olivia" (Stanley's middle-age fiancée) and "Mia," and "Sophie" and "Soon-Yi"? Is this film Mr. Allen's mea culpa—or his apologia—or both? Like the unanswered theological questions posed in *Magic in the Moonlight*, these unanswered biographical questions lie in fallow fields, beckoning seekers and cinephiles to harvest these fallen sheaves.

Mr. Allen's typically eclectic musical choices in *Magic in the Moonlight*—ranging from big-band jazz to Ravel's "Boléro" (yes, the same "Boléro" that was Bo Derek's mid-coital musical preference) to Beethoven's Ninth Symphony—make the movie seem like a lightweight summer trifle. Not that the Ninth is light—its familiar molto vivace movement is especially ominous when used in film; its striking second movement immediately evokes the dark, dystopian denseness of Stanley Kubrick's *A Clockwork Orange* (1971). And the film's rococo backdrops and lush cinematography also lend it a feathery feel. One particular shot, a cinematographic composition of Stanley speaking with Sophie as she sits on a swing in a luxurious garden setting, is an almost exact filmic carbon copy of Jean Honoré Fragonard's rococo masterpiece "The Swing" (1767; oil on canvas; The Wallace Collection, London).

But while the film affects a light appearance, the questions its characters ponder are some of the heaviest dilemmas known to man: Is this all there is? Or is there something more—something beyond what the mere eye can see? Is life "nasty, brutish, and short," as the Hobbes-spouting Stanley likes to state, or is it filled with a mysterious, mystical magic, as the whimsical, waifish Sophie (who is Audrey Hepburn-esque in her diaphanousness) is want to believe? These are only several of the intractable questions that Stanley is compelled to confront, and his reassessment of everything he thought he stood for may have viewers questioning many of their assumptions about God, life, and the universe, or—because it is a non-didactic, nuanced, subtle film with no unitary message—it may not. Like the religious—truth claims of faith, the multiple messages in *Magic in the Moonlight* are conveyed but can never be scientifically proven; it is left up to us to decide whether to take the proverbial leap of faith into the mysterium tremendum and accept them, or to rationalistically remain on materialistic terra firma and reject them.

One of the most salient symbols in *Magic in the Moonlight* is the astronomic observatory. While Stanley and Sophie are driving back from Provence, their car breaks down, and they take shelter in a nearby observatory. It is a place that Stanley used to frequent as a child, he explains to Sophie. When Stanley opens the roof of the observatory so that they'll be able to see the starry night sky, the observatory's magisterial telescope clearly points to the resplendent silver moon crescent.

Stanley, the self-described "sober man of science," flatters himself with this false appellation, for unlike the great astronomers, he is startlingly close-minded in his doctrinaire, unchanging and inflexible worldview. Only when he is with Sophie does he first begin to open the closed roof of the "observatory"—the closed, settled viewpoint of his own mind—to begin to explore what may lie beyond.

In fact, the irony represented by Stanley's affinity for astronomy is illuming: Stanley regards the open-minded religious dolts—the believers in "delusions" who place their chimerical wishes in faith's fraudulent creeds and religions' false hopes—as erring souls. And he perceives the close-minded men of science—those for whom concepts like "belief," "faith," and "spirituality" are irrelevant in a world of empiricism, observation, and experimentation—as the only coterie of humankind in possession of truth. Yet it was the original "sober men"—and women—of science, the great explorers, astronomers, and scientists of years yore who, in their open-mindedness—in their willingness to entertain the possibility that there must be something more than meets the earthly eye, in their belief that there must be something more than this planet, and in their flexibility to integrate new scientific revelations into their old worldviews—opened the knowledge-base of humanity to the wonders of the universe. By pointing the telescope into the sky, the cosmologically curious Copernicus, Kepler, Galileo and Giordano Bruno challenged the close-minded men of medieval religion—the men who believed that this world was fixed and immovable, and that the center of the solar system was our planet—and opened our minds to the awe-inspiring spectacles of this magisterial universe. And it is the cosmologists, astrophysicists, and scientists—those with genuinely open-minded spirits—who continue to push the boundaries of our consciousness by insisting that there is more out there that we do not know, that there are more wonders waiting to be discovered, and that there are more mysteries waiting to be solved. The "observatory," as Stanley subtly indicates, must remain open if we deign to discover the manifold delights of our magnificent material domain.

Chapter Eleven

Inside Llewyn Davis

The Coen brothers are indubitably the most versatile, skillful, and interesting filmmakers in contemporary American cinema. Witness their last five films: *No Country for Old Men* (2007), a flawless,[1] chilling twenty-first century version of *The Night of the Hunter* (1955) which netted the Coen brothers a Best Picture Oscar; the underrated ensemble comedy *Burn After Reading* (2008), a film that features what is arguably Brad Pitt's finest comedic performance since *Twelve Monkeys* (1995); the dark comedy *A Serious Man* (2009), a twenty-first century take on The Book of Job which some critics deemed to be their best film to date—this amongst a filmography that already boasts *Fargo* (1996), *The Big Lebowski* (1998), *Barton Fink* (1991), and *The Hudsucker Proxy* (1994); a virtuosic revival of the Western, *True Grit* (2010); and now, an unclassifiable, confounding tragedy, *Inside Llewyn Davis* (2013), a film that has the feel of a Kafka story (*The Trial*, specifically) transmuted to celluloid.

Inside Llewyn Davis is a leisurely paced tale of the trials and sorrows of a young singer (Oscar Issac) aspiring to carve out a niche for himself in the early 1960's pre-Dylan Greenwich Village folk scene. The film's subdued, unaffected tone, its drawing-room and kitchen-sink scenes, and its adagietto tempo hearken back to the profoundly personal films of the 1970's auteurs, recalling the time when Scorsese, Coppola, Altman, and pre-*Star Wars* George Lucas conveyed personal messages to the film-going public. Except, in *Inside Llewyn Davis*, the Coen brothers have not only made a personal film—they have "done" the personal film before, most recently in *A Serious Man*—but they have gone for something much, much deeper. *Inside Llewyn Davis* is reaching for something very big—a sweeping, existential interpretation of the human condition, perhaps—and the success (if such a term can be used for such a film) of this movie rises and falls with the perception of whether they have attained this result.

The Coen brothers' tragic take on the music movie is a subversive corrective to films like *Walk the Line* (2005), *Coal Miner's Daughter* (1980), and other musician biopics in which the path from a hardscrabble existence to musical success seems predetermined. *Inside Llewyn Davis* reminds us that for every Loretta Lynn and Johnny Cash, there are hundreds of Llewyn Davises. The path to success in the entertainment industry is strewn with the sad tales of those who did not succeed. Llewyn Davis, a character based upon Dave Van Ronk, is one of those figures.

Inside Llewyn Davis holds out the promise of being a unique viewing experience, and it most certainly is. However, this does not mean it offers a pleasing viewing experience. In fact, my initial reaction to the film after leaving the theater was one of visceral dislike; I had never reacted so negatively to any Coen brothers' movie before. And I have seen—and loved— virtually all of their films. What, I wondered, was so unlikable about this particular Coen brothers film?

Some of its unlikability inhered in Oscar Isaac's remarkably pathos-free performance as Llewyn Davis. The character is so devoid of emotion that he seems virtually inhuman. Spending time in the theater with a character as congenitally incapable of caring as Isaac's Davis provokes a reciprocal reaction that makes it difficult to become emotionally invested in the character.

The other reason this film is so unlikable is because it lacks the comedic elements that we have come to expect and enjoy in Coen brothers films. Aside from the hackneyed screwball subplot that involves chasing a runaway cat (a device the Coen brothers previously used in *The Ladykillers* [2004], and one that is also used in Noah Baumbach's *The Squid and the Whale* [2005]), John Goodman provides some of the only comic relief, but mostly as a dialogic symbol of "John Goodman, comic character actor in Coen brothers films." He's not particularly funny in this role, but his mere presence in another Coen brothers film conjures his past performances in Coen brothers films from *Raising Arizona* (1987) onwards, and gives the viewer a kernel of hope that this movie will be like many of the others. It is not.

But mostly, this film is so unlikable because it paints a picture of a world that we would rather not look at; for those of us who have suffered disappointment, heartbreak, and failure—and what human being has not?—it is a picture that may be all too recognizable. Like Kafka's frightening parables about a careless, heartless world, *Inside Llewyn Davis* is an unnerving look at a world with an existential void at its core. It is a film that adopts a fundamentally tragic view of life—but so do many of the Coen brothers' other works, most notably *No Country for Old Men* and *Fargo*. Where *Inside Llewyn Davis* departs from these works is that it is, on the surface, irredeemably tragic—there is no foreseeable saving grace in the world of Llewyn

Davis. It is not only a tragic world, but a Sisyphean one—a cold world without a shred of hope, a lonely world in which we are doomed to a never-ending cycle of disappointment, despair, and defeat. In short, it is the world of Nietzsche's mad- man: it is a world without God.

The great ethico-theological idea that the Hebrew Bible introduced to the world was the idea of a moral God who is involved in the world. As Nahum Sarna observed regarding the biblical monotheistic conception of God,

> The God of the Bible is not a remote deity, inactive and ineffective. Having created the world, He did not remove himself from humanity and leave man to his own devices. On the contrary, He is very much concerned with the world He created and is directly interested in human behavior. [2]

Abraham, the Jewish sages teach, was the first human being to conceive of a personal God: "From the day that God created the world, no one addressed God as 'master' until Abraham addressed God as 'Adonai' [my master]. Abraham saw himself not at the mercy of uncaring Gods but as standing in a relationship with a caring, personal God." [3] Calling God "Adonai," my master, conveys the speaker's belief that God has a personal relationship with each individual. More than steering the world from polytheism to monotheism, Abraham and the monotheistic religions that claim him as their patriarch taught the world that the universe is not a chaotic, cold, hostile arena where people are at the mercy of mercurial gods; instead, the monotheistic faiths portrayed the universe as an intelligible (if not altogether orderly) domain overseen by a personal, loving God. Since the time of Spinoza, the notion of a personal God presiding over an orderly universe has received many blows. These blows first came from philosophy and science, then from literature and psychology, and finally from the behavior of humanity itself. Now, the Coen brothers have demonstrated that film is a medium capable of depicting the consequence of what it means to believe that we live in a world without God.

Llewyn Davis is an unconnected, unmoored, rootless folk singer adrift in an impersonal, uncaring cosmos. Peering down from his squalid Bohemian Greenwich Village apartment, he condescends towards those upwardly mobile, middle-class aspiring persons who do not create and "just exist," but Llewyn barely manages to exist himself. And what kind of existence is his lot? Llewyn exists without a sense of a deeply rooted, venerable past, without a stable community of family and friends in the present, and without an inkling of a hopeful, redemptive future. He is an exemplar of the dreadful Durkheiminan anomie that preys upon individuals who lack the warmth and shared values of a supportive religious community. [4]

One who reaches for too much ends up grasping nothing at all: "tafasta merubah lo tafasta, tafasta muat tafasta," the Talmud states. [5] Immediately after viewing the film, I felt as if the Coen brothers had reached for too much, and had come up empty. But this is not the type of film that deserves a knee-jerk reaction. If one attempts to rapidly consume and digest it like a fast-food entrée, it will not be appreciated. Instead, it should be slowly digested like a complex carbohydrate and processed only after a few days—or even after few weeks.

"You'll have to explain this one to me," a friend I bumped into at the theater said to me after the movie. I'm still not sure I can, but what can be said is that the highly allusive *Inside Llewyn Davis*, in addition to resembling a cinematic version of a Kafka parable, also bears strong resonances of Dante's deeply symbolic *Divine Comedy*. Just as each individual and each episode in *The Divine Comedy* is profoundly symbolic, each individual and each episode in *Inside Llewyn Davis* also carries symbolic weight. For instance, what Llewyn causes his sister to do with his records and memorabilia is analogous to being sprinkled with the waters of the mythological river Lethe in *The Divine Comedy*.

In the Coen brothers' Dantesque film, no creature is more symbolic than "Ulysses" the cat. In many respects, the wandering cat is a feline proxy of Llewyn, and is appropriately named Ulysses.[6] For just as Ulysses was a wanderer, adrift midway through life's journey, so too is Llewyn. Just as Ulysses lacks a true home and community for much of his journey, so too does Llewyn.[7] And just as Ulysses is a crucial figure in Dante's *Divine Comedy* (particularly in the latter cantos of Paradiso) who symbolizes the possibility of redemption—his eventual returning to his home is a microcosmic symbol of the world's eventual restoration to its pure, pre-sin state on a macrocosmic plane—the dual returns of Llewyn and Ulysses the cat to their respective abodes adumbrates the Coen brothers' interest in the redemptive possibility of return and restoration. (The motif of return is operative in *Raising Arizona, Fargo, The Big Lebowski,* and *No Country for Old Men* as well.) Thus, naming the cat Ulysses (who, like the original Ulysses, undertakes an "incredible journey" of its own) serves to evoke the surprising possibility of return and redemption amidst our seemingly hopeless journeys through a cosmos that is, on the surface level, Sisyphean. Furthermore, *Inside Llewyn Davis*'s ambiguous ending conjures the similarly strange ending of Joyce's *Finnegan's Wake* (the nearly impenetrable novel by the author of the modern *Ulysses*): both end where they begin; for both Llewyn and Finn, their nadirs effectuate their eternal Eliadian returns—their ends bring about their recurrent rebirths.

Indeed, almost more than it is a Kafkaesque parable of life in an absurd universe, *Inside Llewyn Davis* is a Dantesque tale of a journey through a hellish environment which culminates in—or at least holds out the hope of—eventual redemption.

NOTES

1. The great artists paint the same picture over and over and over again—Monet and his water lilies, Twombley and his Ledas, Cézanne and his vistas of Mont Sainte- Victoire—until they get it just right; up until *No Country for Old Men*, the Coen brothers had been making movies that were preoccupied with the same concerns—the ambiguity of morality; anomie; existential loneliness—and that featured common motifs—restoration and return; odysseys; folk music; desolate, heartless landscapes; empty roads; terrifying bounty hunters; dimwitted criminals committing bungled crimes—and their experimentations with this form reached its apotheosis in *No Country for Old Men*, in which all of their themes and motifs harmonized to form a filmic masterpiece. (In fact, their usage of the Four Tops song "It's the Same Old Song" in the closing credits of their first feature, *Blood Simple* (1984), contains a line that characterizes nearly all of their subsequent films: "It's the same, same old song / But with a different meaning").

2. Nahum M. Sarna, *Understanding Genesis: The World of the Bible in the Light of History* (New York: Schocken, 1970), 52. See also ibid., 52–58, and Jonathan Sacks "Noach: True Morality," *Covenant & Conversation,* 2012 (positing that the concept of revelation implies objective, universal morality), available at http://www.aish.com/tp/i/sacks/174092141.html.

3. Eliakim Koenigsberg (citing Rabbi Shimon Schwab), "Parshas Lech Lecha—My G-d," *Parsha Bytes,* October 10, 2013, accessed December 31, 2013 http://www.yutorah.org/lectures/lecture.cfm/798650/Rabbi_Eliakim_Koenigsberg/Parsha_Bytes_-_Parshas_Lech_Lecha_-_My_G-d.

4. Émile Durkheim, *The Division of Labor in Society* (1893), idem, *Suicide* (1897).

5. Babylonian Talmud, *Yoma* 80a; b. *Hagigah* 17a.

6. The name "Ulysses" is itself a trope that occasionally recurs in Coen brothers' films; it is the name of the character played by George Clooney in *O Brother, Where Art Thou?* (2000)—a film that exemplifies the Coen brothers' long-gestating interest in *The Odyssey.*

7. Other parallels between Llewyn and Ulysses become illumined upon close watching: Llewyn felt that only his departed singing partner was his musical equal, similar to how Odysseus felt that only "ghosts"—the absent Agamemnon, Achilles, and Ajax—were his "equals." Harold Bloom, *Genius: A Mosaic of One Hundred Exemplary Creative Minds* (New York: Warner Books, 2002), 508. Additionally, Llewyn is accused by Jean (Carey Mulligan) of turning everything he touches into human waste; he can be said to be possessed by some kind of curse. If Llewyn is thought of as an Odysseus, it is interesting to observe that the name "Odysseus" (or "Ulysses" in Latin) refers to one who "inflicts his curse upon others, or someone who himself is victimized by a curse" (Ibid., 505).

Chapter Twelve

All Is Lost

"Fear not:" considering that this imperative is repeated an astounding seventy-five times in the Hebrew Bible it is arguably the single most significant biblical leitmotif.[1] The Hasidic sage Rabbi Nachman of Breslov famously adumbrated this biblical principle with his adage "the entire world is a very narrow bridge, and the main thing is not to be afraid at all." Our Man, the unnamed character played by Robert Redford in J.C. Chandor's remarkable, virtually wordless *All Is Lost*, is a filmic paragon of this biblical maxim. "Our Man"—a name evocative of the primordial biblical (lit., "Man," in Hebrew) of the Bible[2]—is on a small sailboat, dozing in the warm waters of the Indian Ocean, when a stray container of sneakers collides with his boat. Quickly realizing that the cargo container has punctured his sailboat, Our Man devises a makeshift sealant for the hole. All alone on a wrecked sailboat in the middle of the Indian Ocean, Our Man improvises a host of other ersatz solutions and utilizes every ounce of his resourcefulness in his ensuing struggle to survive.

The qualities that are uncanny about Our Man are many, but perhaps the uncanniest quality of them all is his utter lack of fear. He is at times agitated, perturbed, and occasionally extremely frustrated—witness the one-word imprecation he utters during one crucial scene—but he remarkably evinces no fear whatsoever. And neither does he express any degree of self-pity.

In a film season in which the predominant theme has been survival—*Gravity*, *Captain Phillips*, and now *All Is Lost* have all revolved around characters compelled to use every scintilla of energy in order to survive in extreme circumstances—Redford's Our Man is the character tasked with perhaps the most extreme survival trial of them all. Unlike Tom Hanks in *Captain Phillips* and Sandra Bullock in *Gravity*, Redford is truly all alone: he did not embark upon his mission with other crew members, and never has genuine radio contact with another soul once disaster strikes his vessel.

In some respects, *All Is Lost* is in dialogue with *Gravity*—it is, intentionally or not, a companion film to *Gravity*, and these films almost beg to be viewed in tandem. The preferable order would be to view *All Is Lost* subsequent to *Gravity*. *Gravity*'s posture towards silences verges on the hypocritical: Bullock preaches a love of silence, but, along with her co-star, George Clooney, she engages in a near-incessant stream of dialogue.

All Is Lost's genuine silence is a subtle rebuke to *Gravity*'s loquaciousness. And Redford's Our Man is a character with no known backstory, with no words, and most significantly, with no discernible fear—a stark contrast to Bullock's fearful Ryan Stone in *Gravity*. While neither character should be harshly judged for their particular reactions to the extreme circumstances that befall them—after all, one should not judge another person "until you have stood in his place"[3] —Redford's taciturn Our Man is a welcome contrast to Bullock's melodramatic Ryan Stone.

Redford's performance itself is uncanny. Redford is the entire film—it is literally a cast of one. And even though he does not speak but a few words during the film, his performance is anything but one-key: it is modulated and nuanced. Each movement has a purpose, each gesture an aim, and his eyes speak much more profoundly than his mouth ever could; indeed, if one carefully watches Redford's eyes, one will notice a discernable progression in Our Man over the course of the film. That Redford can communicate veritable character development with his eyes alone speaks wonders as to the type of performance he delivers.

Most viewers will come to *All Is Lost* with the knowledge that Redford's character utters perhaps one word of dialogue over the course of the entire hour-and-forty minute film, but like most viewers, I was not truly ready to experience this dialogue-free performance until it was actually occurring in front of us on the screen. *All Is Lost* differs from any other film in recent memory in that it provides us with the visuals but no words, not even via subtitles or title-cards—and is thus even more silent than "silent films"—and, like a novel in which we are provided the words but not the pictures and are invited to stage the visual of the story in our heads, *All Is Lost* compels us to sit back (or, more precisely, due to the story's intensity, to lean forward) and silently script our own versions of Redford's hidden inner monologue.

Redford's Our Man also differs from Bullock's Stone in that Our Man, unlike Stone, expresses no need or desire to pray. Perhaps Our Man prays in his head; perhaps, like Stone, he is frustrated that he does not know how to pray. But he never mentions the word "God," even as an exclamation. Our Man is a hardy soul—after all, one must be supremely self-confident to venture out into the ocean all alone on a sailboat in an attempt to circumnavigate the globe—and one senses that this is not the type of man who would cry out to a higher power as do the sailors in The Book of Jonah. Our Man embodies the maxim of "the matter is dependent upon me alone."[4] He uses the raw materials God has provided him in an attempt to effectuate a miracle of his own making.

While *All Is Lost* is in dialogue with the survival films of this year like *Gravity* and *Captain Phillips*, the survival film it most closely resembles is Robert Bresson's minimalist masterpiece *A Man Escaped* (1956). In Bresson's film, a French POW condemned to death by the Nazis meticulously plots an escape from a prison camp. *A Man Escaped*, like *All Is Lost*, is "unadorned"—there is no score, no subplot, and no hijinks. There is only a man, and all that matters is what he must do to survive. No segment in *A Man Escaped* is superfluous—"I can't think of a single unnecessary shot in *A Man Escaped*," Roger Ebert wrote—and neither is there an unnecessary shot in *All is Lost*. Both *A Man Escaped* and *All Is Lost* are "lesson[s] in cinema."[5]

If one changes "Bresson" to "Chandor," Ebert's description of *A Man Escaped* can easily be applied to *All Is Lost*:

> Robert Bresson's films are often about people confronting certain despair. His subject is how they try to prevail in the face of unbearable circumstances. His plots are not about whether they succeed, but how they endure. He tells these stories in an unadorned style, without movie stars, special effects, contrived thrills and elevated tension. His films, seemingly devoid of audience-pleasing elements, hold many people in a hypnotic grip. There are no "entertainment values" to distract us, only the actual events of the stories themselves. They demonstrate how many films contain only diversions for the eyes and mind, and use only the superficial qualities of their characters.[6]

At a surface level, Chandor's talky *Margin Call*, one of the most underrated films of 2011, seems diametrically opposed to *All Is Lost*'s silence, but one should not conflate dialogue with excess. Every line of dialogue in *Margin Call* is delivered with a purpose, and its method of storytelling is just as spare and simple (but far from simplistic) as the method Chandor employs in *All Is Lost*.

With *All Is Lost*, Chandor has suddenly become one of the most interesting directors working today, and his career trajectory indicates that he could become a modern-day Bresson. In an era in which we are subject to an unremitting barrage of audiosensory stimuli, Chandor's arrival to the directorial circuit is a development that should be welcomed by any lover of quality filmmaking.

NOTES

1. Brettler, Marc Zvi; Enns, Peter; & Harrington, S.J., Daniel J. *The Bible and the Believer: How to Read the Bible Critically & Religiously.* 2012. (New York: Oxford), p. 166.

2. Cf. the tannaitic "our rabbis," a metonym for the rabbinic collective, and "Our Man," a symbol for the human collective will to survive against all odds. "Even when the sword is suspended upon your neck, do not despair from salvation," urges the Talmud (Babylonian Talmud, *Berakhot* 10a), and Our Man never despairs.

3. Mishnah, *Avot* 2:5.

4. Babylonian Talmud, *Avodah Zarah* 17a.

5. Ebert, Roger, 2011. "A Man Escaped," Accessed December 16, 2013.

6. Ibid.

Chapter Thirteen

Reading Movie Reviews as a Religious Experience

Roger Ebert as the Rashi of Cinema

Sometime between the fifth and sixth centuries of the Common Era, the unwieldy corpus of Jewish legal argumentation, rabbinic homilies, and exegetical narratives that had been transmitted orally was transcribed into the text that became known as the Talmud. Despite this successful transcription, for many Jews it remained a closed text—unpunctuated, arcane, and hopelessly prolix. Save for a small cadre of elite scholars, it was still largely undecipherable for most readers until the eleventh century, when Rabbi Shlomo Itzchaki (commonly referred to by his acronym, Ra-Sh-I, or Rashi) began to write his commentary on the Talmud. Rashi's endeavor to make the Talmud accessible to the masses was so fabulously successful that his commentary was selected as one of the two primary commentaries to accompany the Talmudic text in the standard published editions of the Talmud, and is still widely considered well-nigh indispensable in Talmudic studies.

If the canon of cinema were to be transcribed into literary form as the Talmudic text was, and the editors of such an authoritative anthology of film were tasked with selecting two film critics to flank the central film "text," the role of Rashi would indisputably be filled by Roger Ebert.

Just as Rashi's commentary enabled a broader swath of Jewry to study Talmud, Roger Ebert rendered sophisticated film accessible to the masses. And like Rashi, Roger succeeded fabulously, gaining a national following through his syndicated columns and TV show. Just as Rashi's commentary allowed average Jews to navigate the previously untouched waters of obscure Talmudic tractates (and concomitantly established precedents for later Talmudic translations and elucidations, such as today's popular Artscroll edition), so Roger provided moviegoers with entry points into the great undiscovered country of world cinema. His reviews provided the *homme moyen sensuel* with an awareness of the art-house films from Godard, Bergman, Fellini, and Ozu. And because of his championing of independent filmmakers like Scorsese and Coppola, the work of auteurs like Malick and Cassavetes could play in Peoria.

But Roger's and Rashi's non-elitist, accessible commentaries belied their vast intellects; Roger knew his English literature *au fond*, and Rashi's conceptual and analytic abilities were unquestionable. Even though they sought to provide their readers with the simple understanding of film and Talmud, they were by no means simplistic. Their erudition would occasionally slip through in little dollops of aperçus delivered so nonchalantly that insufficiently attuned readers could easily miss them. Roger was a much deeper thinker than he was often given credit for; perceptive readers knew that his conceptual abilities were sometimes obscured by the unfair reputation he garnered from his television show as a shallow "two-thumbs-up" popularizer. Ontological queries were not beyond the scope and ken of a Roger Ebert review: writing about *Eternal Sunshine of a Spotless Mind*, he posited that his intense response to the film may have been due to "my obsession with who we are and who we think we are. The secret of communicating with another person, I suspect, may be in communicating with who he thinks he is." And in his essay on Hiroshi Teshigahara's *Woman in the Dunes* in his 2003 book *The Great Movies,* he pontificated on the meaning of existence, asking "is struggle the only purpose of struggle?"

A Talmud teacher of mine was fond of telling us that there is great wisdom concealed in every comment of Rashi, and he implored us never to "skip a Rashi" lest we miss one of his stiletto-sharp observations. Not only did I adhere to his advice, but upon discovering the Rashi of film, I adapted it to film during my personal cinematic journey. In the thousand-plus films I have viewed, I never "skipped a Rashi." Roger was my cinematic Rashi, and his reviews accompanied each film I viewed as naturally as Rashi's elucidations accompanied each page of my Talmudic studies.

Roger particularly loved *Citizen Kane,* which always retained its "greatest film of all time" status in his mind. The Talmudic apothegm stating that "one who studies a text 101 times cannot be compared to one who studied the text 100 times"[1] could have been said about Roger's relationship with *Citizen Kane*. Just as Talmud students know that they can always come upon a new interpretation of the text in each study session, so could Roger always find fresh insights in multiple viewings of films. Despite 100 (or so) viewings of *Citizen Kane* (including screenings in which he studied it shot-by-shot at film festivals), he was amazed at how he would always find something new that he hadn't observed in a previous viewing. For Roger, film became a text with ever-deepening layers of meaning that only revealed their secrets upon further study.

One of the subjects that most deeply interested Roger was religion, an area he wrote about rather frequently (though he had a knack for doing so in covert as well as overt ways), and in attitudes that alternated between praiseworthy, critical, curious, and admiring. Sometimes the most profound theological statements can be the simplest, and I heard such a statement from Roger at the September 27, 2011, New York TimesTalks Discussion with A. O. Scott: "Since we only live for a short time, we might as well be happy. We have to play with the cards we're dealt. I'm not angry that I got cancer. I'm happy I'm still alive and can keep making people happy."

Roger was and continues to be a loyal cinematic companion for thousands of moviegoers. Although he stated that "[t]he wonder of life and the resources of imagination supply all the adventure you need,"[2] I tend to believe that I speak for many film enthusiasts around the globe when I say that when it comes to the appreciation of film, all you ready is the wonder of life, the resources of the imagination, and the film commentaries of Roger Ebert. Cinephiles will always be eternally grateful for the wealth of wisdom, wit, illumination, and unalloyed enjoyment Roger provided us. It will take some time to come to terms with the sad new reality that films will be released without an accompanying Ebert review; perhaps solace can be taken from perusing the work of the new critics Roger cultivated and brought into his website. Roger's work will be continued by writers whose reviews are suffused with his unmistakable influence. Rashi did not complete his commentary on the Talmud either; others, like his grandson Rashbam, assumed the task of completing his commentary. Yet, because Rashbam's distended, dilated prose was a far cry from the brisk, pellucid style of his grandfather, Rashi endured as the commentator new students of Talmud look to when they begin their journeys into the sea of Talmud. So too, Roger Ebert will always be the quintessential rhapsodist of the movies, and the writer to whom moviegoers turn when they embark on their own journeys into film. Roger's unintentional epitaph, written by him just a day before his death, rings true: "On this day of reflection, I say again, thank you for going on this journey with me. I'll see you at the movies."

NOTES

1. Babylonian Talmud, *Chagigah* 9b.
2. Roger Ebert, "My Neighbor Totoro," *Great Movies*, December 23, 2001, https://www.rogerebert.com/reviews/great-movie-my-neighbor-totoro-1993.

Chapter Fourteen

Hollywood, the Oscars, and the Missing Modern Jew

In four weeks, history will be made in Los Angeles: a man who has never before won the Academy Award for Best Actor will walk home with this coveted Oscar. One possible winner is Christian Bale (who has won a Best Supporting Actor Oscar) for his pitch-perfect performance in *American Hustle*. Another potential winner is Leonardo DiCaprio for his incandescent high-octane performance in *The Wolf of Wall Street*. (If DiCaprio is again denied an Oscar, cinephiles will soon be talking about "Leo's missing Oscar" the same way book-lovers talk of "Philip Roth's missing Nobel.") Bale's and DiCaprio's characters have much in common: they are both avaricious swindlers. But their less obvious—and more troubling—common denominator is that both of these mountebanks are Jewish.

These performances—as fine as they are—are symptomatic of the misleading, incomplete, and at times derogatory images of Jews that perennially emanate from Hollywood. According to the movies, we are either the nerdy, awkward, Herbie Stempel (John Turturro) of *Quiz Show* (1994), trying to move up and out of Bensonhurst and into accent-cleansed, neuroses-free America. Or we are Hyman Roth (Lee Strasberg) of *The Godfather: Part II* (1974) and Sam "Ace" Rothstein (Robert De Niro) in *Casino* (1995), the venal shucksters and shysters whose shenanigans are responsible for the usage of the word Jew as a verb. This year, we have the good fortunate of being treated to a special triple-portion of this variety of Jew: first Meyer Wolfsheim (Amitabh Bachchan) in *The Great Gatsby*, and now Irving Rosenfeld (Christian Bale) and Jordan Belfort (Leonardo DiCaprio).

Or, we are the dithery Alvy Singer (Woody Allen) in *Annie Hall* and the endearingly awkward Greg (Ben Stiller) of *Meet the Fockers*, cowering in shame at the sight of our embarrassingly outmoded parents, fearing for our lives that these squeam-inducing creatures will be the obstacles standing between us and the shiksa goddess. If your parents were Dustin Hoffman and Barbara Streisand, how could you grow up to become anything other than a successfully maladjusted Jewish man?

Or, if we are not the Jews whose Judaism is comprised of guilt-tripping mothers, matzah ball soup, and self-deprecating humor, we are the Jews who wear long beards, side-curls, black hats, white shirts, and long black coats. We are the ultra-Orthodox Jews of *Ushpizin* (2004), for whom the apotheosis of our religion is purchasing an unblemished etrog (a citrus fruit used as a ritual object during the Sukkot holiday), we are Jesse Eisenberg's side-curl-sporting Hasidic drug dealer in *Holy Rollers* (2010), and we are Renée Zell-weger choking under the weight of a stultifying ultra-Orthodox culture in *A Price Above Rubies* (1998). And now we are Shira (Hada Yaron), similarly stifled by the mores of her ultra-Orthodox family in *Fill the Void* (2013).

Rama Burshtein's beautifully shot, carefully wrought *Fill the Void* was Israel's official entry into this year's Best Foreign Language Oscar category. Hada Yaron is marvelous as Shira, the youngest daughter of an ultra-Orthodox family who is under pressure to marry a man not of her choosing. It is a sensitive, artful portrait of the ultra-Orthodox community. But it is only the latest iteration of a film purporting to give us the voyeuristic thrill-ride of peering into a segment of the Jewish community which has already received a surprising number of "inside," "behind the scenes" looks. Films like these further Spike Lee's brief but harmful image of the Jew as a beard-toting, side-lock-curling, black-hat-wearing caricature in the great *25th Hour* (2002, adapted from David Benioff's novel). It is with films such as *Fill the Void* upon which such stereotypes are built, and it is with movies like *Holy Rollers* and *A Price Above Rubies* through which such stereotypes are perpetuated.

It is all well and good that filmgoers have been granted these delectable characters and these wonderful films (I loved *The Wolf of Wall Street*, and believe that DiCaprio deserves to win his first Oscar for his performance as Belfort), but this menagerie of characters are crude caricatures; the Fockers, Hasids, shysters, and nebishy Alvy Singer knockoffs alike are all embarrassingly shop-worn stereotypes. Notwithstanding the Jewish demographic drift towards the poles of assimilationist secularism and totalizing religiosity, a vital center still exists of Jews who practice the laws and rituals that Shira's family observes, but who are simultaneously as much a part of the modern world as are the Fockers and Singers. The Jewish viewpoints on sexuality and women's rights are not exhausted by Shira's ultra-Orthodox family's sacred restrictions and Rozalin Focker's romping libertinism. For modern-observant Jews who acknowledge both of these elements of the sexual experience, Jewish dating and Jewish sex is much more fraught with tension—and much more interesting—than anything we've seen on film thus far (with the exception of *Yentl* [1983] which, if we can be honest, was just plain weird and even mildly disturbing).

Where are the stories of Jews who maintain modern values like the right of a woman to choose a husband while struggling to maintain a tradition in which a canonical text states that "a woman is acquired in three ways: a monetary transaction, a contractual agreement, or sexual intercourse"?[1] The ultra-Orthodox community has had its moment on the screen. Whereof the other Jew, the modern yet religious view, the secular-observant hybrid Jew, the Jew who is equally adept at quoting from the Seinfeld "shiksappeal" episode and from the Talmud? Towards this marginalized Jew who abides in the vital center, "attention must be paid"—a line, of course, penned by a Jew who won himself the greatest shiksa goddess of them all. The missing image of the modern-religious Jew is the real cinematic void that is begging to be filled.

NOTE

1. Mishnah, *Kiddushin* 1:1.

Chapter Fifteen

The Greatest Beauty

The Imaginary Journey of Paolo Sorrentino's
The Great Beauty (La Grande Bellezza)

Sorrentino's award-winning drama opens with a quote from Céline's *Journey to the End of the Night*: "To travel is very useful, it makes the imagination work, the rest is just delusion and pain. Our journey is entirely imaginary, which is its strength."

Jep Gambardella lies on his bed, wraps his arms around his head, and gazes at the ceiling—except he does not see a ceiling, he sees water—cool, shimmering, sky-blue summer water.

We see this striking, almost surreal image several times over the course of Paolo Sorrentino's beautiful *The Great Beauty* (*La grande bellezza*). And there is no more apt adjective for this Best Foreign Language Film Oscar winner, because *The Great Beauty* is quite simply a beautiful film to look at, to listen to, and to ponder.

Jep Gambardella (a wonderful Toni Servillo, looking like a cross between Joe Biden and Bill Maher) is a sixty-five-year-old Italian author whose best days, and best writing, seem behind him. Once the promising young writer of the acclaimed and highly successful *The Human Apparatus*, Jep became content to rest on his laurels and lead the easy life of a classic European *flâneur* (though less a Walter Benjamin-type intellectual *flâneur* than an Italian Jack Nicholson-type *flâneur*) instead of engaging in the difficult task of writing. Having earned enough money from his one hit novel, Jep no longer needs to go out into the court of literature every day, and in Rome— with its great food, nightly parties, uninhibited (or "sophisticated," as a character in a Woody Allen movie might put it) southern European women, endlessly fascinating sights, and infinite opportunities for languid people-watching—why write? If one has the means to enjoy life, and one lives in a city where enjoying life is not a difficult goal to pursue for those with means, why work?

But at sixty-five, Jep seems to be experiencing a mid- (or three-quarters) life crisis. He holds regular gatherings (less salons than they are parties that occasionally involve group discussions) with his clique of mildly successful Italian literati who, except for one woman in the group, have no delusions about their definitively upper-middlebrow status in the world of art. They are content, seemingly, to party away their nights dancing to electronica and while away their days in desultory conversations.

Audiences and critics alike have correctly described *The Great Beauty* as Fellini-esque, for Sorrentino does bathe the screen with the sort of warm, colorful visuals and occasional melancholic tones that are the hallmarks of Fellini's oeuvre. But Sorrentino (who has publicly acknowledged Fellini's influence on *The Great Beauty*) goes a step beyond Fellini; Sorrentino's camera caresses his actors in warmth. None of the actors in *The Great Beauty* could be described as classically beautiful, yet the camera does not shy away from them—instead, it revels in their physical imperfections and tells audiences that we—that everyone, not only conventionally beautiful individuals—all deserve the kind of warm camera caresses (or, in film parlance, to be beneficiaries of "the gaze") typically showered on the flawless, airbrushed beauties of mainstream film. *We* are the great beauties, says *The Great Beauty*—we, in all of our imperfect gloriousness, with all our wrinkles and distinctively shaped features, with all of our different colors and amounts of hair, with all of our height and weight differences—*we*, the real, non-airbrushed human beings, are the true great beauties of this world.

Jep's midlife crisis is provoked by the death of his friend's wife (Elisa), a woman who was apparently Jep's first love. We're given occasional, fleeting, *Marienbad*-esque glimpses into Jep's memory of his first romantic encounter with this young woman. Just as we know something happened between "X" (the unnamed man) and "A" (the unnamed woman) during their stay at the Marienbad resort without ever being quite sure what it was, something of a romantically ambiguous nature was shared between Jep and Elisa one summer near the shimmering, light-blue waters of an idle summer beach.

Sorrentino's camera focuses on Elisa in these cryptic scenes in a way that evokes Alain Resnais's steady focus on Delphine Seyrig ("A") in *Last Year at Marienbad* (1961). Both women exist more in the minds and memories of their spellbound men—"X" (Giorgio Albertazzi, whose character, interestingly enough, is described as "the man with the Italian accent") and Jep—than they do in the objective realities of the respective worlds of both films.

Sorrentino suffuses the screen with other *Marienbad*-esque touches, such as cold, white marble statues, random assortments of well-dressed Europeans gathered inside fine European homes—the sort of homes featuring the end-less corridors and mirrors of the famed Marienbad resort—and a balcony that overlooks a garden very much like the one behind the resort. The sum of these various *Marienbad* influences and motifs creates the impression that we must be just as suspect of the haltingly brief glimpses we're shown of Jep's memory as we are of "X's" account of what occurred between him and "A" (the "brunette") during that strange, shadow-occluded year at Marien-bad.

Nevertheless, it is these vague memories that catalyze Jep's sudden reas-sessment of his life. And his reassessment is also unconsciously provoked by the constant specter of religion that surrounds him and his Roman friends. In very few cities—Mecca and Jerusalem being perhaps the only others—is religion such an integral aspect of the city's culture, society, and structure. Even the irreligious are surrounded by religion; religion is woven into the fabric of the city the way electrical wiring courses through the walls of modern homes and offices. Even if it appears invisible, it is there.

And religion is an overt presence in *The Great Beauty*, largely because the presence of Catholicism is inescapable in Rome. Jep's daily wanderings over and about the city often take him past a convent, and he tends to take his time observing the daily patterns and religious rituals of the lives of some of these nuns in the same manner Japanese tourists in *The Great Beauty* observe the daily patterns and rituals of the lives of Jep and his compatriots.

Jep is brought into even closer orbit with religion when he hosts a dinner for an important Italian cardinal (who, apparently, is not only next in line for the papacy but was also once the country's foremost exorcist) and an ancient Mother Teresa-type saint.

The *flâneur* and the saint; the literati and the clergy; this world and the world-to-come; one senses that Sorrentino deliberately evokes these classic religious contrasts in order to make some sort of statement, or to at least explore the relationship between the artist and the religionist.

How do these seemingly opposing classes of individuals regard each other? At times, they view each other with a "grass is greener on the other side" attitude, and Jep's attempt at a virtuous act—helping out his friend's daughter—may be an admission that he is lacking in virtue, much as the way in which the cardinal rhapsodizes about food may be an admission that he is lacking in certain forms of pleasure (which he attempts to compensate for by reveling in gustatory delights). Yet, despite their brief flirtations with other ways of life and other manners of experience, they ultimately resign them-selves to the lives they have led because they believe they *have* led the lives that are best for them. How Jep and his circle will fill their lives with some sort of meaning and, if they are seeking it, some semblance of hope for the future—something to look forward to beyond sleeping with partners they have yet to sleep with—is unclear. But while one of Jep's friends becomes so disconsolate at his hopeless future that he embarks on a reverse *Cinema Paradiso* (1988) odyssey and leaves Rome to return to his small hometown village (in *Cinema Paradiso*, Alfredo the projectionist memorably advises then-future director Salvatore to head to Rome and leave sentimentality and his village behind), perhaps Jep and most of his circle don't need to look forward to anything. Perhaps the pressing issue in their lives—and the pressing issue in the lives of most artists and non-religionists—is not whether there is anything to look forward to, but how to best experience their existence each day. As Jep intimates toward the end of this story, "looking forward"—viz., heaven—is not the business of novelists anyway. "I don't deal with what lies beyond," Jep says to himself, as if finally arriving at a modicum of emotional and spiritual catharsis. His business is in the telling of stories of human lives in this world, and writers like Jep are needed to perform this service in the best and most beautiful way possible.

And what of the saints? Mirroring Jep, they understand that their business is not in pleasure and riches, so why be envious of what Jep and his friends have had? "We have led good lives, and our business is in other matters," they seem to say. The *flâneurs* and the saints reach a tacit, unarticulated rapprochement: we have radically divergent lives, yet we live together, and we benefit by living alongside each other. We eat together, we party together, we inhabit the same social, cultural, and physical space, yet we are different, and we exult in our differences. Our lives, and the lives of others, are made richer and more colorful *because* we live together while maintaining our distinctive, beautiful ways of life. We are different streams of water—aquamarine-tinged waves and deep-sea-blue tinted waters—that merge in the exquisite shimmering waters of our infinite minds.

Chapter Sixteen

A Movie in the Mold of Murnau, *Metropolis*, and *The Rules of the Game*

Wes Anderson's Grand Budapest Hotel

There may be no more aesthetically sensitive American filmmaker today than Wes Anderson. He lavishes so much love on the look of his actors, sets and costumes that he could be said to be the cinematic heir of Fritz Lang and Stanley Kubrick. He is, of course, not the infamous perfectionist that Kubrick was, nor does not make his actors endure hundreds of takes per shot as did Kubrick and the perfectionist Lang. And neither does his body of work yet rival theirs. But like Lang and Kubrick, Anderson still manages to achieve small perfections in the small slithers of self-sufficient worlds he creates. This petite perfectionism is no more evident than in *Grand Budapest Hotel* (adapted from Stefan Zweig's 1927 novel), a film that approximates the heights of wonderful whimsy that Anderson achieved in *The Royal Tenenbaums* (2001) and *Moonrise Kingdom* (2012).

I do not think it necessary here to discuss the already well-known plot of *Grand Budapest Hotel,* a film inspired by the writings of the Austrian writer Stefan Zweig (1881–1942) and whose droll plot concerns how a young lobby attendant (Tony Revolori) came to be the later proprietor (F. Murray Abraham) of the "storied" Grand Budapest Hotel' in a small fictional Central European state—it involves a disputed will, a priceless Breughelian painting and its Schiele-esque impostor, and a prison escape that involves tiny cupcake cutters used to break down the bars of a prison window (a scene that AO Scott aptly called perhaps "the most Wes Anderson thing ever")—because this is one of those movies that is just begging to be observed and enjoyed regardless of whether one can follow its story.

Again, as in so many of his films, Anderson's set designs are a marvel of imaginative creation. What distinguishes the look and feel of *Grand Budapest Hotel*, though, is its surprising darkness. As in Jean Renoir's great *La règle du jeu* [*The Rules of the Game*] (1939), the frightening reality that the impending outbreak of another world war—and the impending end of a certain European way of life—will soon envelop the sweet, sensual aesthetes and innocuous aristocrats hangs over this film like an ominous storm cloud looming over a stream of innocent Sunday strollers. In creating this feeling of frightening foreboding, Anderson uses the style of Renoir, and—rather appropriately for a film set in 1930's Central Europe—the cinematographic legacies of F. W. Murnau and Fritz Lang.

The set designs Anderson created for some of the movie's darker scenes, and the costumes he created for the eerie Dmitri (Adrien Brody) and the menacing Jopling (Willem Dafoe) owe a significant debt to German Expressionism. With his waxen-faced pallor and his long, tight black outfit, Brody's look evokes Graf Orlok (Max Schreck) of Murnau's *Nosferatu* (1922)—a character, of course, so memorably played years later by Willem Dafoe in *Shadow of the Vampire* (2000). Dafoe's *Grand Budapest Hotel* character— he plays Dmitri's family's haunting hit-man—with his shadowy eyes and coal-black outfit, conjure the mad scientist C.A. Rotwang of Lang's *Metropolis* (1927).

Even though this masterfully made movie and these delightfully dark characters have their macabre aspects, at the heart of this film is a playful lightness and a melancholic love for the lost world in which this lightness flourished. We see the love for this lost lightness when we observe the affection that Anderson lavishes on his actors: look at the way he introduces Edward Norton's character, or the wonderful way his camera winds and weaves with Jeff Goldbum as he walks; and look especially at the way his camera falls in love with one of the most lovable characters Anderson has ever created, the hotel concierge Gustave H (Ralph Fiennes).

This may be Fiennes' finest performance, which is saying a lot when one considers the incredible cadre of characters he has so splendidly played, from the monstrously vile Amon Goeth (*Schindler's List* [1993]) to the amorously virtuous Count Laszlo de Almásy (*The English Patient* [1996]) to the soulful Michael Berg in *The Reader* (2008)—a performance that is easy to overlook because of its understated excellence. But the vainglorious Gustave H exceeds them all.

Gustave H, described twice during the film as "a glimmer of civilization in the barbaric slaughterhouse we know as humanity," is a genuine aesthete the type of which is rarely still seen. He dresses flawlessly, speaks immaculately and carries himself with the same playful dignity regardless of whether he is in a palace or prison. And he is the type of person who, upon escaping from prison, is more concerned with whether his accomplice has brought him the exact kind of perfume he requested (L'Air de Panache, if you must know) than catching the getaway van. Like Thomas Mann's Herr Settembrini in *The Magic Mountain*, Gustave H is an art-loving and poetry-reciting humanistic but is charmingly free of Settembrini's grating pedagoguery. And, as Wes Anderson can be said to be the Oscar Wilde of contemporary cinema, Gustave H is his wonderfully Wildean mouthpiece—a character who lives for art itself, and who lives to please others; Gustave H exists not to edify, but to enjoy.

Gustave's suave gift of the gab is charming to listen to, and his smoothly delivered witticisms are a gift to the thinking moviegoer's intellect. But even more amusing than his verbal acuity is the nuanced acting that Fiennes does with his face. He communicates so many subtleties of feeling and so many intricate inner stirrings with the twinkles of his eyes and with the occasional compression of his lips that there is an entire movie to be watched from observing his face alone.

In the middle of Renoir's *The Rules of the Game*, there is a shot that is so carefully constructed and so perfectly executed that it has been admired for generations as a symbol of cinematographic and actorial excellence. Robert de la Chesnaye (Marcel Dalio), the master of the house of a fading upper-class estate and a collector of specialty music boxes, is displaying his latest piece—the most prized acquisition of his collecting career—to a small audience. When the camera turns from the quirky contraption to Dalio, we see his face: he is joyfully contented, yet unable to conceal the real embarrassment about being so overjoyed. This single ambivalent emotion is communicated in an instant—blink, and you miss it. It is as if the glint in his eyes and the subdued smile of his lips is saying, "yes, I am happy, but can this truly be the apogee of my life? *This*, is my grandest achievement?" According to Roger Ebert, Renoir had to reshoot this scene for two days because Dalio's facial expression had to be just right: "proud, and a little embarrassed to be so proud, and delighted, but a little shy to reveal it. The finished shot," writes Ebert, "is a study in complexity, and Renoir says it may be the best shot he ever filmed."[1]

It has been many years since we have seen a shot like this, but such a shot can be seen at the end of *Grand Budapest Hotel*. When Mr. Mustafa (F. Murray Abraham) tells us that Gustave H remained at the hotel but "did not succeed at growing old," the camera cuts to Fiennes playfully bantering amongst a group of doting admirers, and then zooms in. For a brief moment, we see an actor communicating a range of emotions with his face all in one instant in a manner that has not been seen since the famous shot of Dalio in *The Rules of the Game*. Fiennes' face, eyes and mouth manage to instantaneously express a surface contentment with his life of aesthetic refinement while also implying an abiding sadness lurking in the attic of his heart.

And this, indeed, is the overriding sentiment we feel when watching *Grand Budapest Hotel*: the same sentimental sensation of a silent mourning for a lost, lovely, refined way of life that Renoir's *The Rules of the Game* articulated is imparted by Anderson in *Grand Budapest Hotel*—but without Renoir's sly social satire. Anderson does not seek to critique or to edify; rather, he seeks—in an almost Wildean sense—to please, and in a Debussy- or Satie-esque way, to stir the emotions. This is the effect that the looming darkness and the subtle sadness of *Grand Budapest Hotel* has on us: it is such a beautifully amusing film, so wonderfully acted, and so carefully designed, that the fact that we know that the refined, sensitive, humanistic pre-war European world it portrayed would soon come to an end fills the mind with tears of tragedy. There is so much lovely melancholy for this enchanting lost world seeping out of *Grand Budapest Hotel*'s screen that your heart is rended and your spirit weeps when watching it. Like Dalio in *Rules of the Game*, and like Gustave H in *Grand Budapest Hotel*, we walk away from Wes Anderson's wonderful film with a look of pleasurable contentment on our faces for having enjoyed such a charming movie while being unable to conceal the tragic sentimental melancholy we feel floating up from our hearts and invading our souls.

NOTE

1. Roger Ebert, "The Rules of the Game," *Great Movies,* February 29, 2004, https://www.rogerebert.com/reviews/great-movie-the-rules-of-the-game-1939.

Chapter Seventeen

The Big Short

The Big Short is a choppy, entertaining, and frustrating movie all at once, but its most distinguishing feature is what it says about morality: that is, the lack thereof in the financial system of the USA. Based on the best-selling book by Michael Lewis of the same name, and written and directed by Adam McKay, a comic filmmaker known for *Anchorman* (2004) and *Talladega Nights* (2006), *The Big Short* tells the story of the Great Recession of 2008 through the eyes of a few intrepid traders who saw the financial collapse coming—and made hundreds of millions by betting that the collapse would happen.

In an Oscar-nominated performance, Christian Bale plays an extremely intelligent, extremely introverted doctor-turned-trader who foresees the coming collapse of the housing market and, to the great chagrin of his boss, "shorts" (that is, bets against) the likelihood that millions of Americans will continue to be able to pay their mortgages. A panoply of other players show up in various roles: some (Brad Pitt) are disaffected with the system, some (Ryan Gosling) enthusiastically embrace it, and others (a foul-mouthed, brilliant Steve Carell) are deeply conflicted. But one way or another, they all end up either profiting from the crash, or—like Pitt's character—helping friends profit from the economic plight of others.

McKay also brings in celebrities for educational purposes, having Margot Robbie in a bubble-bath explain subprime lending, Anthony Bourdain in a restaurant kitchen explain Collateralized Debt Obligations (CDOs) by analogizing them to fish stew, and Selena Gomez (along with the renowned economist Richard Thaler) at a Las Vegas blackjack table explain "synthetic CDOs." And this is the general tenor of the movie: flashy, tongue-and-cheek, economically esoteric and deadly earnest all at once.

The Big Short succeeds at telling the terrible story of how millions of Americans lost jobs, homes, pensions, and retirement savings in the greatest financial collapse since the Great Depression. Even though the director draws too much attention to himself with ostentatious camera movements, lighting-quick cuts, and far too much use of the close-up (for some reason, nearly the entire movie is shot in close-up, with choppy, handheld camerawork to boot, making for a jittery, dizzying viewing experience), this hard-to-watch film is a must-see movie. It will be remembered as one of the most important—but not one of the best—films of this decade not only on account of its dramatic portrayal of a few of the individuals who were instrumental in causing and profiting from the Great Recession of 2008, but because of what it revealed about the stunning lack of morality, religious-based ethics, and basic human compassion in our economic system.

In a country as religious as the United States (roughly seven-in-ten Americans identify as Christian, according to the latest Pew survey; over eighty percent of Americans identify as religious; and only 3.1% of Americans identify as atheists), it is devastatingly disappointing to see just how little moral compunction the bankers portrayed in *The Big Short* possess. *The Big Short* holds up a mirror to the face of our financial system and shows it to be the whited sepulcher of the Gospel of Matthew: a world that is "beautiful on the outside, but on the inside is full of dead men's bones and everything unclean" (Matthew 23:27). The world of finance is a world of glitzy, high-priced office-buildings on the outside, but on the inside is full of corruption, greed, and economic sin. It is a world where economic utility, crass self-interest, and simple greed have replaced religious ethics, age-old morality, and simple human compassion. In this economy, the primacy of monetary relations have overtaken moral relations. Cold, heartless economic calculations have overwhelmed intuitive interpersonal kindness. "Woe unto you, scribes and Pharisees, hypocrites!" one wants to scream at the Wall Street bankers who stole from the poor to give to the rich, "don't you know that one cannot serve both God and mammon?!" As Moses L. Pava, Professor of Business Ethics and Dean of the Sy Syms School of Business of Yeshiva University, has observed: Extreme forms of free market ideology, which have permeated the culture of global finance and economics, and have come to dominate, if not monopolize business and political discourse, come perilously close to a kind contemporary and everyday idolatry.

And as the philosopher Kenneth Seeskin has noted: Although many people still think of God as a man on a throne, idolatry in the modern age is generally considered a moral error rather than an intellectual one. If God is the only thing in the universe worthy of worship or adoration, then anyone who becomes obsessed with the desire for wealth, beauty, fame, or power is said to idolize them. From a modern perspective then, idolatry is a universal phenomenon. Almost every country in the world has military parades that glorify power, advertisements that glorify beauty or sexual fulfillment, books that extol wealth or influence, and cults that deify movie stars and sports figures.[1]

If McKay's movie—and Lewis' book—is a journey into the center of our finance-based economic system, then the terrifying reality they have discovered is that lying in our economy's heart is pitch-black idolatrous darkness. "The horror, the horror!" we exclaim in our hearts upon viewing a world where the vain seek vanity, the greedy lust after lucre, and the governmental guards, who were supposed to prevent the powerful from abusing the needy, abandoned their posts; some even joined in the fray, fecklessly frolicking in the pursuit of the fleeting goods—and false gods—of this world.

After seeing *The Big Short*, one will no longer wonder why so many millions of Americans have flocked to the upstart, rebellious campaigns of Donald Trump and Bernie Sanders this election season. The sense of anger that so many of us have against those who cost us jobs, homes, pensions, savings, and our belief in the viability of the American dream is real. But the cure for our broken country and corrupted economy isn't just to stage a political revolution or build a wall—what first and foremost must happen is a restoration of ethics, morality, and basic human compassion into the heart of our economy and into the hearts of every banker and financier, every woman and man: "And you shall love the Lord your God with all your heart, and with all your soul, and with all your strength. And You shall love your neighbor as yourself. There is no other commandment greater than these" (Matthew 12:30-31). If we can accomplish this, the day will soon come when we can all proclaim loud and clear: "Mistah Corrupt financier—he dead."

NOTE

1. Kenneth Seeskin, *No Other Gods: The Modern Struggle Against Idolatry* (West Orange, NJ: Behrman House, 1995), cited by Moses Pava in "Everyday Idolatry and the Ideology of Free Markets" (forthcoming article).

Chapter Eighteen

La La Land

Movie of Dreams

The two movies that squared off against each other for February's Oscar for Best Picture could not be more different. The first contender, *Moonlight*, is a moving, grimly realistic film directed by Barry Jenkins about a young man's struggles to come to terms with his sexuality and his identity as he comes of age in a difficult, drug-infested region of Miami. The second contender, *La La Land*, is a bittersweet, delightfully fantastic musical directed by Damien Chazelle about two young artists (Emma Stone, playing an actress, and Ryan Gosling, playing a pianist) struggling to realize their dreams in a city (Hollywood) that crushes more dreams than it fulfills. *La La Land*, filled with catchy music, exhilarating dance numbers, and a gorgeous color palette, is a charming, at times enchanting diversion that is an homage to the good old-fashioned *Singin' in the Rain*-style escapist Hollywood musical. *Moonlight* is almost the dictionary-definition—if such a thing exists in the movie dictionary (perhaps there's an entry for this term in Roger Ebert's old *Little Movie Glossary*)—of an "anti-escapist" film: it is completely authentic in every way imaginable. *La La Land*, in what immediately became the most famous moment in the history of the Academy Awards, was mistakenly announced as the 2017 Oscar Winner for Best Picture, but it was *Moonlight* that actually walked home with this most coveted of all movie industry awards.

La La Land (spoiler alert) ends with a whimsically conceived "alternate ending" in which everything works out perfectly for Sebastian and Mia—but of course, in the "real life" of the movie, it doesn't: Sebastian and Mia don't live happily ever after together. Life, as the film knows so well—and so beautifully and touchingly depicts—inevitably disappoints. Even if it seems as if things do turn out happily ever after in *La La Land*—Mia lands her dream career and a loving family; Sebastian gets his dream job—the alternate ending reveals that they both would have been much happier if they had stayed together and had worked toward their respective dream careers while supporting one another. But it didn't happen—they drifted apart. The real did not live up to their ideal.

This is why *La La Land* is one of the greatest films of recent memory: it humanely affirms the universal human element of inevitable sorrow and disappointment that is at the heart of all our enterprises. Beneath the perfunctorily cheerful, contented exterior that society usually compels us to don like a too-tight-fitting clown mask is an interior welter of melancholy and sadness. Lift up these masks and you can glimpse the silent, secret mourning that—save for a few rare individuals—we each engage in on account of the loss of our dreams, our vanished hopes, and our unfulfilled desires. We are each capable of so much, and each of us desires to do so much, but the harsh limits of life ineluctably constrict our possibilities. The sages of the Talmud understood this well, acknowledging that "no person dies having fulfilled half his desires."[1] One may have desired to be an art gallery owner living in a three-car-garage house San Francisco; when one instead ends up a schoolteacher living in a three-bedroom apartment in New York with a compatible spouse, even though it seems like everything has "worked out" for this person on the surface, deep down lies a reservoir of suppressed sadness on account of not having achieved one's desires. Our personal happily-ever-after ending hasn't been fulfilled, and we silently mourn, in the recesses of our minds, over our unfulfilled desires—silently and privately, because it is not considered socially acceptable to be sad when it appears to others as if one is fulfilled. And yet we are not fulfilled—most of us who appear to have stable jobs and steady relationships actually carry a real sense of melancholy with us which we're afraid of expressing because it won't be validated as a "worthy" type of sadness to have. Henry David Thoreau aptly encapsulated this acute psychological predicament when he famously wrote, "[t]he mass of men lead lives of quiet desperation and go to the grave with the song still in them"[2]—our desperation is "quiet," because to others it would seem petty to talk about one's sadness over not having become that star sports announcer or best-selling cookbook author one dreamed of when one has a stable job as regional sales manager for a national department store chain. Sadness is permitted for those who have suffered major, *Manchester by the Sea*-scale tragedies, society tells us, not for those have endured minor *La La Land*-type sorrows.

What is worse is that because of our infinite imaginative capacities it is so easy for us to visualize the ideal alternative to our present lives—the dream job, the perfect partner, the romantic reunion with the high school sweetheart. Whatever it is we desire, our minds concoct lush, vibrant fantasies for ourselves, much like the alternate ending constructed for Mia and Sebastian in *La La Land*. That our real lives almost never measure up to our ideal lives—and the silent sadness on account of these unfulfilled hopes that we are so skilled at suppressing—is as much a part of real life as is anything else.

We hope and dream for something wonderful, and this dream is so tantalizingly real that, like Mia and Sebastian, we can picture it happening in all its technicolor vividness, only to have this beautiful dream crushed, shattered by the cruel imperfections of mortal life.

And then, at the Oscars, life imitated art in the most surreal of ways imaginable: *La La Land* was announced as Best Picture Winner. Everything works out perfectly: the beautiful dream is made real, the impossible hope comes to fruition, the—no . . . of course the beautiful dream wasn't real. It never was. It was always too fantastical to be true. The ending in which *La La Land* wins Best Picture was the too-perfect "alternate ending." In reality, things don't work out: dreams are shattered; hopes are crushed; earthly imperfections overtake imagined wonders.

But we smile, if we can, at those (like the *Moonlight* cast and crew) for whom it does somehow miraculously work out, and take solace in the fact that we have art—our hopes, our yearnings, and our impossible, unrealizable dreams that, as Henry James wrote, complete (but do not represent) our incomplete lives—for just such moments.

NOTES

1. Kohelet Rabbah 1:13. Cf. Rabbi Moshe Chaim Luzzatto, *Mesillat Yesharim* 11:151.
2. Henry David Thoreau, *Walden* (New York: Barnes & Noble Classics, 2003), 11.

Chapter Nineteen

Blue Jasmine

The fallen woman: it is a common trope in tragic metatheatre [1] (think Tennessee Williams's Blanche DuBois in *A Streetcar Named Desire*, or the type of character that Ibsen's women are desperate to avoid becoming), and is also a recurrent historical phenomenon (think Marie Antoinette). The fallen woman is not as common of a trope in religious literature, but Cate Blanchett's mesmerizing performance as Jasmine in Woody Allen's *Blue Jasmine* (2013) is redolent of a relatively unknown female character from talmudic lore, Marta bat [the daughter of] Baitus. During the Roman siege of Jerusalem prior to the destruction of the second Temple in 70 C.E., provisions understandably began to dwindle, and Marta, one of the wealthiest Jerusalemite women, asked her servant to procure fine flour. Unable to find fine flour, the servant returned, saying only white flour remained. Marta asked him to buy white flour, but when he arrived at the market, the supplies of white flour had been exhausted, and only dark flour remained. She asked him to buy dark flour, but when he returned to the market, the dark flour had also been exhausted. Marta then asked him to find barley flour, but even this type of flour was unavailable. Thus, not bothering to even put on shoes, Marta hurriedly went out herself to see if she could find any food; she subsequently stepped in excrement and died from the trauma. When he heard about this event, Rabban Yoḥanan ben Zakkai intimated that Marta's story was a fulfillment of the toḥakhah [the biblical prediction of curses that would befall people in calamitous times]: "The tender and delicate woman in your midst who would not deign to traverse barefoot upon the ground" (Deuteronomy 28:56). [2]

Marta's story is a tale that could be told in any age, and Woody Allen tells it with distinctively twenty-first century flourishes. While never quite reaching the desperate circumstances of the Talmud's Marta, Allen's Jasmine nonetheless faces a similar plight. Sundered of her wealth and privileged lifestyle (she was married to a financial tycoon who was implicated in fraudulent schemes and, like Bernie Madoff, had his entire fortune confiscated by the government), Jasmine is compelled to exit the posh confines of Edenic Park Avenue and make her own way in the Californian wilderness. She leaves New York—not exactly barefoot, as she was able to retain her Luis Vuitton luggage and various sundry accoutrements—for San Francisco, where she is not so destitute as to be seeking barley flour in the marketplace, but is seeking her sister in the vicinity of Market Street.

Jasmine's precipitous fall from wealth (which may also be characterized as a fall from grace, given her troubled mental state, her assumption of heavy drinking, and her overreliance on medication) obliges her to move into her sister Ginger's (Sally Hawkins) "homey" apartment that Jasmine, in her previous incarnation as a Park Avenue socialite, would likely have described as a slum. From there, she sets out to commence a new life, and a slew of tumultuous events ensue.

The startling (and, to many of Allen's fans, disappointing) discovery that *Blue Jasmine* is not a comedy has been well-documented; it is a tense, interior, psychological drama that invites viewers to indulge in cinematic schadenfreude by voyeuristically gazing at the rude awakenings delivered by a harsh world to the formerly pristine, utterly spoiled woman who once "threw the best dinner parties" on Park Avenue. (Jasmine was the type of woman whose husband would, like Richard Burton would do for Elizabeth Taylor, give her a "£127,000 diamond ring simply because it was Tuesday."[3] Though not as dark or noirish as *Match Point* (2005), and not as broodingly Bergmanesque as *Interiors* (1978), *Blue Jasmine* is nevertheless far removed from a conventional "Woody Allen film"; though it still possesses an essential comedic core, and while it contains sufficient doses of Allen's trademark neurotic brand of humor (as well as his standard jazz score), it is essentially a comedic drama that verges upon tragedy. And as a slightly humorous moral fable that elicits genuine ethical questions, the Allen film with which it is most analogous is his masterpiece—and the film with which he seemed to invent his own cinematic genre, the "tragicomic wisdom film"—*Crimes and Misdemeanors* (1989). The ethical dilemmas in *Blue Jasmine*, though, are largely retrospective—filmgoers will wonder whether Jasmine acted appropriately during her years of luxury, rather than pondering whether a character's prospective course of action is ethical (as one does when viewing *Crimes and Misdemeanors*).

Contrary to some critics' hyperbolic, reflexive proclamations of this entrée being Woody Allen's best film, *Blue Jasmine* never reaches the cinematic perfection of *Match Point* or the sublime inventiveness of *Crimes and Misdemeanors*; nor can it compare with the uniqueness of *Manhattan* (1979), the comedic brilliance of *Annie Hall* (1977) and *Hannah and Her Sisters*

(1986), or even with the imaginative feats of *Midnight in Paris* (2011). But it is one of Allen's most nuanced, subtle, and complex films, and it may contain the greatest performance he has ever elicited from an actress—which is saying a great deal, given that his direction has produced 11 best actress or supporting actress Oscar nominations. All of the performances in *Blue Jasmine* are full of wonderful brio, especially Sally Hawkins's Ginger, Andrew Dice Clay's Augie, and Bobby Cannavale's Chili, but none more so than Blanchett's Jasmine.

Blanchett has acknowledged that her character is based upon Blanche DuBois—with dollops of Ibsen and Shakespeare—and it seems as if she particularly molded her Jasmine after Vivien Leigh's Blanche in Elia Kazan's 1951 adaptation of the Williams play. (Cannavale's Chili also appears to be riffing on Brando's immortal Stanley.) But Blanchett somehow makes Jasmine even more layered, deep, and complex: Jasmine is also a compelling combination of Bronte's Jane and Bertha, a veritable female Jekyll and Hyde in her vacillations of mood. One can dare say that Blanchett's performance in this film will be spoken of in the same breath as Bette Davis's in *All About Eve* (1951), Elizabeth Taylor's in *Who's Afraid of Virginia Woolf* (1966), Meryl Streep's in *Sophie's Choice* (1982), and only a select few others in an elite category of all-time great performances by an actress.

It is fitting that *Blue Jasmine* showcases such a stellar performance, for it is a film that is fit for the stage. Allen's film also evinces shades of Eugene O'Neill's confrontational, pathos-ridden metatheatre, and Arthur Miller's tragic subversions of the American Dream. "Go west, young man—didn't Horace Greeley say that?" Jasmine asks, before learning that perhaps she hasn't gone far west enough. (Greeley technically did say "Go West," and probably popularized the expression, but he did not coin phrase.[4]) The American dream is as chimerical for Jasmine as it was for Biff and Willy; her story speaks to them through the theatrical ether, informing them that even if they had gone west—to a ranch to work in the open air, or even as far west as Alaska—their existential quandaries would still be unresolved. In her diasporic existence in the West, Jasmine seeks to maintain a veneer of haute couture, but her former social integuments have all but dissolved. She behaves and speaks in a slyly condescending manner to Ginger—and especially toward Ginger's friends—but this new social circle exhibits a charming, if uncouth, bonhomie that her previous social circles lacked.

In addition to his expected theatrical and literary references, Allen also appears to reference a film that one would not expect: Brian De Palma's *Scarface* (1983). In one of her forays with Ginger into San Francisco proper, Jasmine encounters Chili and Eddie, whose attempts to talk to her are reminiscent of Tony's and Manny's initial awkward attempts at talking to American women at the Floridian beach. The fiery Chili's (Bobby Cannavale) interchange with the cool Jasmine evoke similar scenes between Pacino—the hot, mercurial young go-getter full of machismo—and Pfeiffer—the slightly older, standoffish, icy Hitchcock Blonde. Chili's friend Eddie (Max Casella) provides some comic relief (that a Woody Allen film requires comic relief is itself indicative of how much of a *Match Point*-esque genre departure this film is for Allen); Casella plays Eddie as a spitting image of Joe Pesci.

Still, the essential filmic prerequisite for appreciating Allen's *Blue Jasmine* is Kazan's *Streetcar*; one is tempted to say that it should be required viewing for *Blue Jasmine* filmgoers, much as Marbury v. Madison is required reading for Constitutional law students, or as Stravinsky's Le Sacre du printemps is required listening for students of modernist music. Jasmine's melodramatic mood oscillations, Chili's brutish mannerisms, the claustrophobic mise en scène, and Jasmine's dependence upon the kindness of strangers all have their origins in Kazan's adaptation of the Williams play.

Blue Jasmine is not Allen's greatest film; a dubious deux ex machina inserted toward the film's dénouement is fatal for its pretentions of reaching the summit of Allen's considerable oeuvre. Yet, it is a tremendous cinematic achievement for a 77-year old writer-director whose perceptive "eyes have not dimmed, nor has" his passion for film or directorial "strength diminished" (Deut 34:7). In fact, Allen's directorial powers seem to have increased since he withdrew from acting in his own films; such an artistic triumph is a theological reminder that, though the Creator may be hidden, he still abides as an indubitably influential Force in his Creation.[5]

NOTES

1. See Susan Sontag, "The Death of Tragedy," in *Against Interpretation and Other Essays.* (New York: Farrar, Straus and Giroux, 1961).

2. Babylonian Talmud, *Gittin* 56a.

3. Chris Williams, ed. *The Richard Burton Diaries* (New Haven: Yale University Press, 2012), 209.

4. "Horace Greeley," *New York Times,* accessed August 8, 2013. http://topics.nytimes.com/top/reference/timestopics/people/g/horace_greeley/index.html.

5. See Irving Greenberg, *For the Sake of Heaven and Earth: The New Encounter between Judaism and Christianity* (Philadelphia: Jewish Publication Society, 2004), 52; cf. B.T. *Yoma* 69b (arguing that God's power is most keenly sensed in His hiddenness rather than in His overt miraculous interventions).

Chapter Twenty

The Wolf of Wall Street

"One who loves money is not satisfied with money," states the Bible in Ecclesiastes 5:10. When the rabbis of antiquity expanded upon this apothegm and wrote, "envy, desire and greed remove a man from the world,"[1] this may as well have been a Delphic utterance about Jordan Belfort. Martin Scorsese's latest masterpiece, *The Wolf of Wall Street*, is at once a brilliant display of virtuoso filmmaking at its finest, as well as a cautionary tale that illustrates the biblical and religio-ethical warning concerning the perils of unchecked greed, envy and desire.

Jordan Belfort was clearly one for whom the admonition "don't be greedy, for a greedy person is an idolater, worshipping the things of this world" (Colossians 3:5) was not a living value. In real life, Belfort was one of the most notorious white-collar criminals of the past thirty years, and was the King (or "Wolf") of Wall Street until a long-simmering FBI investigation finally dethroned him and put him behind bars. The fraud prince of penny stocks penned *The Wolf of Wall Street*, an eponymously titled memoir about his avaricious exploits, while stewing for several months in federal prison. After a similarly long-simmering production process, Leonardo DiCaprio, writer Terence Winter, and director Martin Scorsese finally brought a film about this devilishly duplicitous yet irresistibly charismatic figure into the light of day and onto the light of cinema screens.

DiCaprio dramatizes Belfort's deviousness so effectively, so mercilessly, and so dynamically, that DiCaprio's Belfort takes on mythic hues. DiCaprio's Belfort is greedier than Michael Douglas's Gordan Gecko (*Wall Street*, 1987), more animalistically lustful than Marlon Brando's Paul (*Last Tango in Paris*, 1972—or Brando's Stanley Kowalski [*A Streetcar Named Desire*, 1951]), and more incorrigibly covetous than Cain (Genesis 4) and Kane (*Citizen Kane*, 1941, from Orson Welles).

Like Charles Foster Kane, Jordan Belfort could have led a simple life
with a modest income and a happy wife, and like Kane, Belfort was a man of
outsized ambitions but without the ethical scruples of a moral tradition or a
religious discipline that could have helped him harness his hubris. Belfort, as
portrayed by DiCaprio, does not possess the patience to toil away in the back
alleys of Wall Street finance firms, and when the company for which he was
working suffers through the Black Monday stock market crash of 1987 and
lays off much of its workforce—including him—Belfort is fortuitously yet
unfortunately provided with an opening to indulge his amoral ambitions.

While job-hunting for stock-trading jobs, he chances upon a shabby
stock-trading shop in Long Island. What it lacks in glamor and glory, it
makes up for in entrepreneurial opportunity. Belfort is at first surprised to
become appraised of what the firm does—selling artificially inflated penny-
stocks to easily manipulable men and women—and that it may not be so,
well, legal. But he becomes intrigued when he is informed that a trader can
net a seemingly infinitely greater commission on selling penny-stocks compared to the infinitesimal commission he had been earning as an honest
salesman of solid stocks on Wall Street.

"Let me give it a shot," he asks the penny-stock traders. He picks up the
office phone, makes a few calls, and within minutes he has miraculously sold
a small-fortune of penny-stocks. The other traders are so awestruck by his
overwhelming penny-stock- selling performance that they are rendered
dumbstruck. It's as if they're the baseball scouts watching a young Roy
Hobbs (Robert Redford) throw fastballs across a tawny Midwestern corn-
field, or a comedy-club audience watching a young pre-*Seinfeld* Jerry Seinfeld perform a stand-up set. Belfort is not just a natural; he could be the
greatest salesman of all time. If a salesman is only out there "on a smile and a
shoeshine," as Willy Loman would have it, DiCaprio's young Belfort is out
there on a smile as scintillating as the light of a thousand suns, and with a
shoeshine that could make the grimiest coal-miner's loafers glow like green-
and-white gold.

Belfort soon realizes that he has the talent to go out on his own. He opens
up his own penny stock-trading company, brands it with the faux-respectable
name "Stratton Oakmont," and recruits a home-grown crew of his own to
join him. When he's finally joined by the audacious Donnie Azoff (Jonah
Hill) and begins collecting obscene (yet not quite enough—never quite
enough—for him) gobs of money, he finally becomes "the Wolf of Wall
Street."

But Belfort does not only live for money—he's just as addicted, if not
more so, to drugs and sex, and he and Azoff use their illicit earnings to fuel
their drug-induced Quaalude-crazes and their profligate patronization of
high-priced prostitution. Lest we think that Belfort was originally destined
for this degree of depravity, the film informs us that he had the chance to take

a different, more upright route, if not for having been taken under the wing of a fabulously foul-mouthed trader played by a scene-winning Matthew McConaughey. The masterful two-minute monologue he delivers to DiCaprio in the five- star Wall Street restaurant may be the film's crucial scene, for it is here where we learn how the callow Belfort became so corrupted, and it is here where we learn that Belfort then deigned to become this devilish apprentice.

It is an origin story akin to the one Milton appended to Satan, and indeed, one must turn to the Satan of *Paradise Lost* to find a villain as compelling, alluring, and irresistibly seductive as DiCaprio's Belfort. But one must also turn to religion to find a puissant discipline sufficiently capable of controlling con men as slippery as Satan and Belfort.

But Belfort not only lacks any discernable ethical code and moral scruple; he even lacks the self-awareness and the reflective capacities to heed the early warnings of the FBI agent (Kyle Chandler) to cease his sinful ways. The agent's investigations should have served as sufficient admonishment, but Belfort's Ahab-like obtuseness in ignoring the agent's Elijah-esque implorings imperils Stratton Oakmont, and he persists in his avarice until it is too late to save himself and his friends from their self-inflicted doom.

Scorsese's latest film—yet another monumentous cinematic achievement in a career marked by many magnificent movies—certainly has its detractors, and they have pointed to the film's seemingly excessive and allegedly gratuitous depictions of Belfort and his company's flamboyant, lascivious lifestyle. The movie does feature inordinate amounts of sex, crudeness, and lewdness, but the blatant bacchanalia serves a purpose; like Hieronymus Bosch's vivid depiction of the agonies of hell in *The Garden of Earthly Delights* (oil-on-wood; 1504), we need to see the full degree to which Belfort and his company flaunted their wealth in order to understand the depths of their depravity. By focusing on Belfort's bottomless depravity in such a deep and sustained way, we are able to truly see the deleterious consequences of greed, envy, and unchecked desire.

Belfort is a hopelessly ambitious and incorrigibly restless character, and his greed, desire, and lack of self-control eventually compromise his friends, his marriage, and his very life. His satanic enthusiasm is seductively contagious, and his lavish lifestyle may be attractive, but in the end, because he cannot contain his greedy desire, it devours him alive. As Scorsese himself says about Belfort, "the devil comes with a smile."[2]

NOTES

1. Mishnah, *Ethics of the Fathers* 4:21.

2. "Martin Scorsese Defends 'The Wolf of Wall Street': 'The Devil Comes With a Smile' (Q&A)," *The Hollywood Reporter,* December 31, 2013, accessed January 24, 2020, https://www.hollywoodreporter.com/race/martin-scorsese-defends-wolf-wall-667851.

Chapter Twenty-One

Museum Hours

In a quiet section of the Galleria Doria Pamphilj in Rome—a lesser-known Roman art museum in comparison to the Vatican, but nonetheless one which should not be overlooked--hang four small Pieter Bruegel paintings. They are closely grouped together, and can be easily missed; each one is only slightly larger than the size of a typical laptop screen, and they are four of the most exquisite, stunningly detailed man-made creations one will ever see. If the import of the anthropo-theological doctrine of *imago Dei* [*tselem Elokim* (in Hebrew)] is substantive—that is, if human beings possess some of the capacities of God—Bruegel's paintings are among the best pieces of evidence attainable that testify to the claim that human beings possess a scintilla of the creative capacities of the Creator of the universe.

A veritable Bruegel bonanza is evident in contemporary independent film; in the niche, rarified world of artistic cinema, two films about the same artist within two years of each other could legitimately constitute such a craze. 2011's awesome ("awesome" used in the genuine sense of the term) *The Mill and the Cross,* from director Lech Majewski, used the mise en scène of Bruegel's "The Way to Calvary" (1564) as the film's *point de repère*. It not only used the painting's backstory as the source for the film's narrative, but also essentially attempted to submerge audiences into the world of the painting itself.

That over two hours were required to tell the story of only one Bruegel painting is indicative of the complexity of his paintings; each one contains a Dickens novel. Anyone who has gazed intently upon a Pieter Bruegel painting in a museum knows that it is terribly easy to lose oneself in the painting; the Flemish master's complex, intricate, extraordinarily detailed artworks appear to contain entire worlds. Just as early cinema studies recognized the proto-cinematic qualities of Dickens's narrative technique—jump-cuts, the

skillful interweaving of multiple storylines, and a large cast of colorful characters are merely some of the prominent "cinematic" features of Dickens's
novels—it appears as if filmmakers are at last stumbling upon the proto-
cinematic qualities of Bruegel's paintings.

In *Museum Hours,* director Jem Cohen does not frame an entire film
around a single Bruegel painting; instead, Bruegel's paintings are the muses
that inspire the film's story. Cohen focuses upon an Austrian museum guard
Johann (wonderfully underplayed by Bobby Sommer) and his love of art—
especially his affection for Bruegel—and his brief encounter with a Canadian
woman, Anne (played by the singer Mary Margaret O'Hara). They meet in
Vienna's storied Kunsthistorisches Museum, where Johann introduces Anne
to the work of Bruegel and acquaints her with the rest of the museum. Over
the course of their platonic relationship (Johann is gay), they visit some of
the city's other tourist attractions, and Johann helps Anne cope with the
emotional burden of being the sole family member tasked with caring for a
hospitalized cousin.

The kind of chance encounters with which Bruegel's paintings are suffused—the same sort of encounters one finds in Dickens's novels and in real
life—lend the film's motivic notes a tenor of providential euphony. Bruegel's paintings also thematically overlay the film's illustration of the random
events—such as Johann's and Anne's serendipitous encounter—and the
physical paraphernalia that constitute the ephemera of the mundane. *Museum
Hours* uses the filmic medium to articulate that such objects and events are
precious enough, and sufficiently intricate, to comprise an eternal work of
art, just as Bruegel used the artistic medium to express this same sentiment.
In this regard, Bruegel's paintings and Cohen's film adumbrate the perennial
existential concern of religion: how we lend meaning and significance to our
lives. Religion often does so by ritual; in religions with conceptions of heavenly reward and punishment, each action, according to such creeds, will be
requited with appropriate compensation in an afterlife. Such notions serve to
eternalize the ephemeral by construing each action as cosmically consequential. For other religionists, everyday life is imbued with sanctity when the
structuring myths of religion are imposed upon existence. Art imparts meaning to the mundane by transforming simple street-scenes into eternal works
of art: seemingly anodyne occurrences—spilt milk, frolicking children, gos-
sipers, haggling vendors—were transfigured into brilliant visual fabliaux by
Bruegel hundreds of years ago, and can still be seen by viewers today.

Bruegel's art and Cohen's film both manage to evade the predicament of
artistic·detachment.[1] Bruegel's artistic life and artistic creations were inti-
mately bound up with those around him; far from depicting flawless creatures frolicking in Arcadian vistas, Bruegel's paintings showcase a bouquet
garni of seemingly unheroic images from everyday life that constitute the
heroism of the *homme moyen sensuel.* Cohen's film imitates Bruegel's art in

its similar evocation of empathy for ordinary human beings: just as Bruegel chose to paint poor peasants rather than aristocrats, wealthy merchants, or mythical beings, Cohen's unglamorous film is so devoid of movie-star luminosity that it even deploys a nonprofessional actor (Sommer) in its leading male role. Both *Museum Hours* and its artistic muse visually convey the transcendent value of individuals—including underappreciated museum guards—as beings who are *imago Dei,* and who thus deserve artistic focus in accordance with their status as beings created in God's image.

The film itself is slow, lyrical, and melancholic; its deliberate pace conjures a *mono no aware* sensibility (defined by Roger Ebert as the receptivity to the "bittersweet transience of all things"[2]) that is rarely felt outside of Japanese cinema. Its weakness, however, lies in this same meandering tempo from which it gleans some of its uniqueness. Its desultory sections beg for just a soupçon of judicious editing (some of O'Hara's singing seemed gratuitous), yet not too much, for among its strengths is its Bruegelesque, halakhicesque attention to the sundry details recorded by Cohen's roving camera—from lost mittens, discarded shopping bags, and an assortment of tchotchkes strewn across the Viennese streets to its score-less soundtrack that implicitly encourages viewers to refine their visual acuity and concentrate on each individual's facial expressions, behavior, and body language (one shot contains perhaps the most accurate visual description of how a museum can trigger adolescent boredom).

Yet, despite its meandering pace, like a painter taking her time to observe her work from a distance before returning to it, and like a digressive preacher's sermon that somehow winds its way back to its message—like a plane that languidly hovers over its final destination before its pilot finally guides it in for a landing—Cohen's film eventually proceeds toward a tranquil consummation. *Museum Hours'* purpose, though, is not the deliverance of a message, but to decant the sensation that "it is not anything transcendent that creates holiness but rather the visible reality"[3] of life in all its details. Much as Bruegel's paintings transformed the overlooked detritus of everyday life into eternal works of art by integrating them into his paintings as *objets trouvés*, and analogous to religion's ability to transform mundane ephemera into sacred ritual objects, Cohen's film illuminates the preciousness of the ordinary. Just as Bruegel's art was overlooked in his own time, *Museum Hours* and *The Mill and the Cross*—in spite of each work's current status as a *succès d'estime*—did not garner wide attention upon their initial releases. But, as those who later discovered Bruegel's magnificent artworks as resplendent artistic masterpieces that contained secret messages (as does the Book of Daniel, according to biblical scholars) and hidden meanings[4] and concomitantly evoke the infinite value, equality, and uniqueness of every human being, the hidden cinematic gems of *Museum Hours* and *The Mill and the Cross* may eventually be uncovered as filmic treasures that do not "wink at us from 'beyond' like" stars that sparkle "in the distant heavens," but are entities which appear to us "in our actual, very real lives."[5]

NOTES

1. Artistic detachment has its religious corollary in the detachment from concrete reality that certain modes of religiosity can engender; cf. David Hartman, with Charlie Buckholtz, *The God Who Hates Lies: Confronting & Rethinking Jewish Tradition* (Woodstock, VT: Jewish Lights, 2011), 132–157, and Judith Plaskow, *Standing Again at Sinai: Judaism from a Feminist Perspective* (New York: Harper & Row, 1990), 62–70.

2. Roger Ebert, "An Autumn Afternoon," 2011. Accessed Sept. 13, 2013. http://www.rogerebert.com/reviews/great-movie-an-autumn-afternoon-1962.

3. Joseph Soloveitchik, *Halakhic Man* (Philadelphia: Jewish Publication Society, 1983), 21.

4. Jeroen J.H. Dekker, "A Republic of Educators: Educational Messages in Seventieth-Century Dutch Genre Painting," *History of Education Quarterly* (1996): 155-182; Walter S. Gibson, *Pieter Bruegel and the Art of Laughter* (Berkeley and Los Angeles: University of California Press, 2006), 10.

5. Soloveitchik, *Halakhic Man,* p. 36.

Chapter Twenty-Two

Life Itself

Life Itself, documentarian Steve James' adaptation of Roger Ebert's epony-mously titled memoir, is a touching, entertaining, and often difficult movie to watch. As his devoted fans, longtime readers, and many others knew, Ebert's last several years on earth were enveloped by a crippling struggle with cancer of the jaw. Several complicated surgeries temporarily checked the cancer's growth without entirely eradicating it. Ebert eventually lost his physical mo-bility, most of his jaw, his ability to speak, and his ability to eat and drink. In his last few years of life, Ebert subsisted on a diet of liquids and puréed food fed directly into his esophagus through an intravenous tube and a suction mechanism. In the documentary's most difficult scene to watch, we even see an example of how this feeding was accomplished.

Observing Roger's suffering (and hereinafter I will call him Roger, for all his longtime readers—myself included—always felt like we knew him on a personal level), and especially thinking about it in the context of his erstwhile television combatant (and eventual dear friend) Gene Siskel's brain cancer, inevitably conjures the question of theodicy: why do bad things happen to good people? Why would a benevolent, omnipotent, omniscient God (assum-ing, arguendo, that these are our theological premises) let such unfortunate fates befall individuals who gave so much pleasure to so many people? If we believe in an authoritarian, strict-disciplinarian God, what could poor Roger have possibly done to deserve such a malevolent malady? To adequately explore the theodical issues implicated by James' film would exceed the scope of this review. However, these issues should not—nay, *can* not—be ignored by any thinking theologically-oriented cinephile. I defy any lover of Roger's writing (or, for that matter, any compassionate soul) to watch the scene of Roger being fed through a suction tube and not inexorably question either God's benevolence, omniscience, or omnipotence.

Even though Roger lost his ability to speak, he did not lose his ability to write. And, like Stephen Hawking, he was even able to "speak" through a computerized voice by typing into a voice-enabled computer. His last few years were a triumph of his—and the human—spirit. He grew more silent, but because of his pioneering use of social media (he was an early adopter of blogging, Facebook, and Twitter), he reached wider audiences and communicated with more people than ever before.

Because he shot *Life Itself* during Roger's last five months of life, James, the director of the groundbreaking 1994 documentary masterpiece *Hoop Dreams*, a film which Roger championed when it was inexplicably neglected by Oscar voters, understandably fills a great portion of this film with scenes, stories, and reminiscences of Roger's final, illness-plagued years. In a society such as ours in which illness and death are often outsourced from our homes as well as from our minds, these scenes are important to see. However, the majority of Roger's life was cancer-free; thus, the ratio of illness-to-non-illness scenes feels out of whack. *Life Itself* is weighted down by an excessively skewed focus upon the illness-encrusted portions of Roger's life.

When James does focus on the majority of Roger's rich, lively life, the documentary is enlightening, entertaining, and religiously illuminating. Roger, we learn, grew up as a single child in a small town in Illinois. He displayed a propensity for writing from an early age. He wanted to go to Harvard, but because his parents told him "there is no money to send you to Harvard," he went to the University of Illinois. Perhaps this twist of fortune was providential, for at Illinois, he was given a prominent platform at "The Daily Illini," and was then plucked by the Chicago Sun-Times for a plum entry-level newspaper position immediately upon graduating college.

Roger never set out to be a movie critic. He was an English major at Illinois, and was considering undertaking doctoral work in the subject. He began his Sun-Times tenure as a sportswriter, and was given the movie beat simply because there was no one else there who was doing it. (Before Roger was given the job, their movie reviews were often written by Mae Tonée—that is, "matinée," meaning whichever Sun-Times writer happened to be going to the movies that afternoon.)

Even though writers like Pauline Kael and Andrew Sarris were beginning to elevate film criticism to the level of an art-form, writing about the movies was still not regarded as a journalistically prestigious endeavor. Roger Ebert, though—with the help of Kael and Sarris, of course—changed all that. Roger signaled that he would be joining the Olympian ranks of those eminently esteemed critics when he accomplished a feat that not even Kael nor Sarris had achieved; in 1976, he became the first writer to win a Pulitzer Prize for film criticism. But unlike the more intellectual Kael and Sarris, Ebert was a populist. He believed that all films, even the great art films of Bergman, Antonioni, and Fellini, belonged to the people. And he believed that everyone should be able to appreciate and understand a film. As A.O. Scott astutely commented, Roger's writing was always clear and compulsively readable, but even though his writing betrayed the wide learning and nuanced analysis of a sophisticated thinker, he never pandered or condescended to his audience.

He was a non-apologetic partisan of the cinema who wrote about the movies from a place of love, not—contra far too many critics—from a place of jaundiced jadedness. When he doled out a bad review (as he was more want to do in his early than later years), he did it not out of contempt for the movie or the filmmaker but out of disappointment; he sincerely wanted to feel the sense of wonder from the movies, that *mysterium terribile et fascinans* [1] —that inexpressible feeling of awe and transcendence that is constitutive of the religious experience—which made his movie-going a pseudo-spiritual, numinous experience.

Roger's most religious reviews ("religious" in this Ottonian sense), from Kubrick's *2001: A Space Odyssey* (1968) to Terrence Malick's *Tree of Life* (2011), exult in emotions of awe and transcendence at the mystery of existence and the wonder of the universe.

Roger was raised Catholic, and he eventually abandoned the jejune faith and conventional religiosity of his childhood. However, he retained an irrepressible interest in Catholicism throughout his life. In fact, one of the reasons that Roger championed (and was perpetually fascinated by) the work of Martin Scorsese—a reason James' film does not mention—is because Scorsese (a fellow Catholic) dramatized the very same crises of conscience, tortured attitude toward sexuality, and ineluctable sentiments of guilt that Ebert may have experienced himself. Witness his "Great Movies" essay on Scorsese's *Mean Streets* (1973):

> Martin Scorsese's "Mean Streets" is not primarily about punk gangsters at all, but about living in a state of sin. For Catholics raised before Vatican II, it has a resonance that it may lack for other audiences. The film recalls days when there was a great emphasis on sin—and rigid ground rules, inspiring dread of eternal suffering if a sinner died without absolution. [2]

One month before his death, Roger summed up his faith thusly:

> I consider myself Catholic, lock, stock and barrel, with this technical loophole: I cannot believe in God. I refuse to call myself an atheist, however, because that indicates too great a certainty about the unknowable. [3]

Catholicism was the subtle, substantial strain of thought that always subsided in the substratum of Roger's work and life. Shakespeare's history plays consciously distanced themselves from their sources—the ideologically tinged historiography and Anglocentric narrative of Holinshed's and Halle's histories—without wholly abandoning the "Tudor myth" and the weltans-chauung of English exceptionalism.[4] So too, Roger distanced himself from the traditional theological truth-claims of Catholicism without entirely ex-punging the emotional elements of the religiosity which he absorbed in his childhood.

Towards the end of *Life Itself*, Roger says that the specter of death did not disturb him because, as someone who was raised Catholic, he had heard about death all the time. Religion has historically been much more adept at administering the *memento mori* than secularism; traditional religion espe-cially excelled at reminding mankind of its mortality. In ancient times, Eccle-siastes advised that "it is better to go to a house of mourning than to a house of feasting, for death is the destiny of everyone; the living should take this to heart" [7:2]—or, as Heidegger, would have it, if we want to experience "*eigentlichkeit*," if we want to be truly alive, we should spend more time in graveyards and less time with "*das Gerede*," the hollow prattle of cocktail parties, the dull droning of infotainment, the insipid babble of "reality" tele-vision, and other such fearful phenomena of Salingerian phoniness. And in modern times, Billy Graham's message, says Professor Robert P. George, was "as simple as it was powerful: Our lives on earth are short. Soon enough each of us will die. Do you want to go to heaven? Then you must give your life to Christ. . . . Quoting Scripture, he would say, 'Now is the accepted time; today is the day of salvation.'"[5]

To a large degree, *Life Itself* functions as a secular, film-length *memento mori*. It reminds us all that, like Roger, "[e]veryone shares the same fate—the righteous and the wicked, the good and the bad" (Ecclesiastes 9:2); it causes us to contemplate what Thomas Mann (in *The Magic Mountain*) termed the "transcendent strangeness" ("*unvergleichbaren Eigentümulichkeit*") of death; and it beckons us to ask ourselves whether we are spending our brief sojourns on earth in the most valuable ways possible.

Since Roger's passing, no one has yet emerged to fill the position of preeminent populist American film critic that Roger vacated. A.O. Scott comes close, but he can be a bit too intellectual for the *homme moyen sen-suel*. Roger's passing has left a void in my life as well. I have yet to find a critic whose writing resonates with me as profoundly as Roger's did on every level. I have yet to find a critic whose reviews I read religiously—that is, a critic whose reviews I feel I must read because they are so influential that they function as canonical commentaries on the films. I miss Roger's "Great Movies" essays, his *Citizen Kane* film commentaries, and his ardent admira-tion of Michael Apted's *Up* series—the series that you, Roger, so aptly called "the most noble use of film" that you've ever witnessed. I miss your enthu-siasm for the horizon-expanding potential of the great science fiction film; I miss your rational, reasoned, learned, and always enthralling takes on relig-ion. I miss your blog; I miss your Midwestern, all-American wholesomeness and the unadorned, pellucid prose style of the Chicagoan that you were; and I miss your paradoxically (yet consistently) high-minded attitude toward art, always insisting that video games were not, and could never be, "art." I miss the way you raised our collective literacy with the literary references you embedded in your reviews. I miss the way the movie-lover that you became was first and foremost a book-lover at heart. I miss the way you wrote about reading for pleasure, and I miss the way you steadfastly believed in the value of being well-read, even in this fast-paced, technologically obsessed infotainment age—an era that is enshrouded in information but shallow in wisdom. I miss the way you said "books do not furnish my office; *they furnish my life.*"

I miss your weekly Friday reviews, your yearly top-10 lists, and your annual post-Oscar column. I miss your movie dictionary, your Answer Man column, and your social media posts. I even miss the yellow background and red typeface of your old website. I still can't believe that we won't be hearing from you when the new Malick, Scorsese, and *Up* movies come out. I miss you, Roger. And, as always. . . . I'll see you at the movies.

NOTES

1. Rudolph Otto, *The Idea of the Holy, An Inquiry into the Non-rational Factor in the Idea of the Divine and Its Relation to the Rational*, trans. John W. Harvey (Oxford, 1923), pp. 29–30.

2. Roger Ebert, "Great Movie: Mean Streets," Rogerebert.com, December 31, 2003, accessed January 7, 2015, http://www.rogerebert.com/reviews/great-movie-mean-streets-1973.

3. Ebert, "How I am a Roman Catholic." 2013. Roger Ebert's Journal, March 1, 2013, accessed January 7, 2015, http://www.rogerebert.com/rogers-journal/how-i-am-a-roman-catholic.

4. Michael Neill, "Henry V: A Modern Perspective," in The Folger Library Edition of *Henry V* (New York: Washington Square Press, 1995), 253–278, at 253–4, referencing E. M. W. Tillyard, *Shakespeare's History Plays* (London: Chatto & Windus, 1943); and Lily B. Campbell, *Shakespeare's Histories: Mirrors of Elizabethan Policy* (San Marino, CA: Huntington Library, 1947).

5. Robert P. George, "The Evangelist" (review of *America's Pastor: Billy Graham and the Shaping of a Nation*, by Grant Wacker), in *The New York Times Book Review*, December 21, 2014, p. 14.

Chapter Twenty-Three

Theotropic Motifs in *Gatsby*

The Cinematic Illumination of a Biblical Theology

Young readers of the Narnia novels may not intuit that the series is an extensive religious allegory, but upon discovering Narnia's theological underpinnings, it is difficult to read these novels without seeing their theological motifs. While most novels are not consciously written as religious allegories, some seem more susceptible to theological readings than others, and *The Great Gatsby* is such a novel. Baz Luhrmann's winning adaptation of Fitzgerald's classic brings the novel's implicit anthropopathic resonances to such salience that one could almost believe that F. Scott Fitzgerald had taken a page out of C.S. Lewis's religious repertoire and written an allegorical novel called *The Great Gatsby*.

The Great Gatsby's overt theological theme lies in the self-evident and much-noted parallel between the eyes of Dr. T.J. Eckleburg and the eyes of God, both of which "always watch over" their respective domains, in accord with Deuteronomy 11:12: "The eyes of the Lord your God are always upon it (the land)." However, the novel contains a more significant, if implicit, theological leitmotiv that is revealed when it is refracted through the prism of anthropopathic Old Testament theology.

An expansive literature on anthropopathic theology exists, and its parameters are still being delineated by theologians, biblical scholars, and ethicists; perhaps most pertinent for this chapter is David R. Blumenthal's articulation of this theology as signifying the Personhood of God:

> Since personhood is the core of our being and since we are created in God's image, God must also have personhood. In anthropopathic theology, God has a Face and a real Personal Presence or Personality. To put it formally: person-

hood, with its expressions as face, presence and personality, is God's, and we
have that capacity because God has created us in God's image.[1]

If biblical theology is anthropopathic—that is, if the God of the Bible is
conceived of as having a personhood that closely approximates the personhood of human beings—the biblical love story between God and Israel can
be much more easily grasped. This chapter posits that an interdisciplinary
approach to theology—reading the Bible through the lenses of literature and
film—can increase our understanding of biblical anthropopathic theology,
and suggests that a theological reading of *The Great Gatsby* can significantly
increase our appreciation of both the classic novel and of the contemporary
film *Gatsby*.

Much as Kant's *Critique of Pure Reason* produced a "Copernican revolution" in Western Philosophy, Abraham Joshua Heschel's *The Prophets* stim-
ulated a similar anthropocentric paradigm shift in biblical theology. Whereas
theology since the medieval era conceived of God as transcendent, perfect,
and lacking nothing, Heschel's *The Prophets* revealed the God of the Old
Testament to be anthropapathic, needy, and profoundly lacking in a very
human way: God lacks a loving relationship, and desires man to freely join
Him in a covenantal relationship.

Heschel carried this theological discovery to its logical conclusion in *God
in Search of Man,*[2] famously arguing that the Old Testament demonstrably
shows that, as much as man needs God, God needs man, and more than man
searches for God, God searches for man:

> Most theories of religion start out with defining the religious situation as
> man's search for God and maintain that God is silent, hidden and unconcerned
> with man's search for Him. . . . To Biblical thinking, the definition is incom-
> plete and the axiom false. The Bible speaks not only of man's search for God
> but also of *God's search for man.* "Thou dost hunt me like a lion," exclaimed
> Job (10:16). . . . This is the mysterious paradox of Biblical faith: *God is
> pursuing man.* . . . All of human history as described in the Bible may be
> summarized in one phrase: *God is in search of man.*[3]

Heschelian anthropopathic theology has become so pervasive in current
Jewish thought that its resonances are even felt in Orthodox theology. For
instance, Lord Rabbi Jonathan Sacks writes, "God does not impose his presence on humanity. Only if we reach out to Him do we find Him reaching out
to us."[4] Such statements may be read as representations of traditional Jewish
theology, but are in fact evocations of Heschel's paradigm-shifting theology
that overturned a millennium of Jewish medieval theology and resuscitated
the biblical conception of God as in need of man.

If Heschel had emulated C.S. Lewis by penning an allegorical novel
whose theological motifs are only discernible to those equipped with the

requisite religious sensibility to glimpse them, *The Great Gatsby* would have been that novel. The pathos-ridden story of Jay Gatsby's laborious efforts to regain Daisy Buchanan's love evokes the covenantal model of divine and human love inherent in Heschelian theotropic biblical theology. Daisy (played by Carey Mulligan) is courted by a character (Leonardo DiCaprio's pitch-perfect Gatsby) whose éminence grise (the Jewish Meyer Wolsheim) is implicated in businesses of ill-repute; in *An Education* (2009), Carey Mulligan's Jenny (in what is still her best screen performance to date) is courted by David Goldman (played with the ideal mixture of allure and cunning by Peter Sarsgaard), a Jewish character involved in nefarious business dealings. And in *Wall Street: Money Never Sleeps* (2010), Mulligan plays Winnie Gekko, the daughter of Michael Douglas's Gordon Gekko, the cinematic archetype of financial corruption. While Gekko's ethnicity is ambiguous (though the character is reputedly based upon the Jewish junk-bond king Michael Milken and the Jewish insider traders Ivan Boesky and Carl Icahn), Douglas's is not—he is half-Jewish. Even more strangely, Winnie Gekko's fiancée Jacob Moore is played by the ethnically Jewish Shia LaBeouf. Viewers will draw their own conclusions as to the either coincidentally trivial or oddly troubling pattern of these roles. Viewers of *Gatsby* and readers of *The Great Gatsby* will similarly draw their own conclusions as to whether Fitzgerald's novel is best read as a theological allegory—an allegory which cannot objectively be said to have been intended by Fitzgerald, but which can nonetheless be adduced as a subjectively legitimate hermeneutic in conceptualizing this literary work.

In covenantal courtship, "[b]ecause the potential vassal . . . must *choose* to accept the latter's yoke, the suzerain must *woo* his vassal."[5] Analogous to Gatsby's need to court Daisy, the anthropopathic God, desiring a covenant with man, must court, or "woo," Israel. Like Gatsby's elaborate, elongated courtship of Daisy, God's courtship of man is also a rather attenuated process—but, whereas Gatsby's courtship of Daisy takes years, God's courtship of man requires eons. Over the course of nearly fourteen billion years,[6] God created a vast, wondrous universe, and over the course of nearly four billion years, God used evolutionary mechanisms to create man, eventually endowing man with intelligence (a process that itself took a millions of years), all so that man would perhaps seek Him. Similarly, as Jordan explains to Nick, "Gatsby bought that house so that Daisy would be just across the bay."[7] Over the course of several years (which are thousands of years in "God-years," as Psalm 90:4 states: "a thousand years in Your eyes is like a day"), Gatsby amassed a great fortune, "had waited five years and bought a mansion where he dispensed starlight to casual moths,"[8] threw all of his ostentatious parties, all so that *she* might "'come over' some afternoon to a stranger's garden" to seek *him*. Gatsby was hidden to Daisy but, like God, was actually everywhere, surrounding her, trying to envelop her: "In 'hiding,' the Divine was calling on Israel to discern the Divine, which was hidden but present *every-where.*[9] All that God wants from us, after all of His efforts in constructing a universe and in creating mankind, is that we should seek Him: how can we also not be shaken by "[t]he modesty of the demand"?[10]

And why does God exert Himself so mightily in his efforts to woo us? Why does Gatsby go through a five-year long rigmarole to lure Daisy? Because, just as Gatsby needs Daisy, "God has need of man."[11] Why does God need man, and why does Gatsby need Daisy? Because they both need love, which is the only thing that all of their might, wealth and power cannot coerce: "Without man's love God does not exist as God, only as creator, and love is the one thing no one, not even God himself, can command."[12] Without Daisy, James Gatz would not have become Jay Gatsby: she was the catalyst for his astounding transformation. And if Gatsby cannot reclaim Daisy's love, all of five years of hard work, scheming, and strategic court-ship[13] will have been for naught. Gatsby strives so mightily to reclaim her love because without it he would not exist as Gatsby. Likewise, according to Old Testament covenantal theology, if God cannot win man's love, all of His work in building the universe and in creating man will have been in vain.[14]

Gatsby, like God, is an elusive, mysterious character with a vague iden-tity—we know as little about God as the partygoers at Gatsby's fêtes knew about Gatsby—and, like God's emanation from His hiddenness (*hester* [Heb.]), Gatsby emerges from amidst this penumbral seclusion in order to seek Daisy. When man is unresponsive to God's persistent courting, God may deign to send oblique yet unmistakable messages that He is seeking man: "Every day a heavenly voice resounds from Mount Ḥoreb,"[15] according to the rabbis.[16] Similarly, Gatsby calls out to Daisy every night through his luminous mansion and fabulous parties, desperately seeking to draw Daisy to him by way of sheer magnetism. When man fails to respond to these signs, as Daisy fails to respond to Gatsby's signals, God uses prophets to deliver messages to man, as Gatsby uses Nick to reach Daisy. And when man re-mains deaf to these messages, God, in desperate need to reach man, resorts to revelation—such as the monotheistic revelations of Sinai, of the person of Jesus Christ, and of the angel Jibril to Mohammed—but such revelations are seldom experienced in history, much as Gatsby's revelation to Daisy only occurs after a significant amount of time and effort. Such an anthropopathic reading of Fitzgerald's novel makes it eminently clear that, just as "[t]he Bible is a record of God's approach to His people,"[17] *The Great Gatsby* may be read as the story of Gatsby's approach to his beloved Daisy. Whilst many films, poems and novels may be read in this vein—the biblical book *Song of Songs* is a prime example of a love story to which anthropopathic and alle-gorical readings have adhered—Fitzgerald's novel, particularly when read in conjunction with viewing of Luhrmann's filmic adaptation, is particularly amenable to a theological reading, for seldom does a literary narrative so prominently feature a love story whose protagonists so closely align with the personas of the anthropopathic biblical God (as does Gatsby) and the equivocal, vacillating biblical Israel (as does Daisy).

The theotropic[18] allegory of *Gatsby* is even more apparent in the explicit divine metaphors that Fitzgerald grafts onto his protagonist. The young James Gatz possesses the confidence to recreate himself as Jay Gatsby because of his belief that "he was a son of God";[19] Luhrmann's screenplay has Nick exclaiming that Gatsby has "more money than God";[20] and when Gatsby kisses Daisy for the first time, he knew that "his mind would never romp again like the mind of God. . . . At his lips' touch she blossomed for him like a flower and the *incarnation* was complete."[21] Since not every line of the novel is recited in this film adaptation (though many are), Luhrmann's editorial selection of these particular theological expressions—in addition to ascribing a divine appellation to Gatsby of his own accord—ensures that the theological motifs in Fitzgerald's novel which are discoverable when the novel is read with a theological hermeneutic are not lost on viewers of *Gatsby.*[22]

These theological motifs are brought into even starker relief upon viewing how the God-like Gatsby, though endowed with "more money than God," cannot buy Daisy's love with spectacular display after spectacular display, just as the God of the Bible could not buy Israel's love with miracle after miracle; God only wins Israel's love when she grants full consent to God at Sinai by exclaiming, "everything that God has said, we will do and we will hear [*nishmah*]."[23] Just as "the commandment to love is the only one God cannot enforce,"[24] Daisy's love is the only object that Gatsby cannot buy. Both God and Gatsby undertake elaborate love conquests not only because they cannot buy their paramours' love, but precisely because their objects of desire are themselves worthy—at least in the eyes of God and Gatsby—of such conquests.[25] These paramours cannot buy their lovers' love from an ontological perspective, and neither can they do so from a romantic perspective: Israel and Daisy must remain autonomous if their love is to be valued by God and Gatsby. God desires a covenantal relationship of love predicated upon equality,[26] and Gatsby desires a relationship in which Daisy can freely and genuinely profess her complete love for Gatsby.

In a love story that is tantalizingly similar to biblical covenantal theology's dialectic between theonomy and heteronomy,[27] Gatsby comes tantalizingly close to winning Daisy's love, only to fall agonizingly short of attaining it in the climactic Plaza Hotel suite scene. In some ways, Daisy is more akin to the post-Sinaitic biblical Israel—the Israel who never completely loves God but is instead forever, in the unforgettable locution of the King James Version, "whoring after other gods" (*Judges* 2:17), forsaking the "love of her youth" (*Jeremiah* 2:2); Daisy forsakes Gatsby, the "love of her youth," and, at least in Gatsby's mind, goes "whoring after other gods"—the gods of old money, complacency, and security. Daisy does profess her love of Gatsby in the sinaitic Plaza Hotel suite scene, but admits that she still loves Tom. Gatsby cannot tolerate Daisy's syncretistic love of both him and Tom; for Gatsby, Daisy must love only him, echoing God's demand for Israel's complete and total fidelity: "thou shalt have no other gods before me" (Exodus 20:3). When Gatsby realizes that he has asked too much of Daisy and the edifice of his dreams is revealed to be a mere façade, he exhibits such a frightful display of vengeance that he looks "as if he had 'killed a man.'"[28] Similarly, when Israel—even at the foot of Sinai—cannot renounce their love for other gods, God (through his avatar Moses) lashes out at Israel by smashing the tablets of the Ten Commandments into pieces in a fashion that seems to prefigure Luhrmann's dramatic exegesis of Gatsby's frightful glare.

Daisy's relationship with Gatsby was never the same after the Plaza Hotel incident, and neither did Israel's relationship with God ever completely recover after this post-Sinaitic trauma. According to rabbinic-midrashic imagination, Israel was never able to fully experience God's glory after the first Tablets were shattered. Why this was thought to be so may relate to the mystical conception of Torah as the embodiment of God: "God, Torah, and Israel are one."[29] According to an Idelian reading of talmudic thought, the primacy of Torah study in the rabbinic tradition ("the study of Torah is equal to all [of the commandments]"[30]) may be informed by the mystico-theological view that the words of Torah are the essence of God; thus, to study the words of Torah is to commune with God Himself. Midrashic literature accordingly endows the first Tablets with the healing properties of gaze that are typically attributed to gods[31] : because the first Tablets symbolized the unsullied, pristine relationship between God and Israel, the Torah—that is, God—could be instantaneously understood by a mere glance at the words of the Tablets. The second Tablets, by contrast, symbolized the fragmented relationship between God and Israel; hence, painstaking effort was required to comprehend the Torah—that is, to see God. To this day, rigorous Torah study is, for better or worse, a *sine qua non* of religious praxis in normative Judaism—a requirement that, according to the Talmud, was neither inevitable nor held to be a religious desideratum: "Had the first [set of] tablets not been shattered, the Torah would never have been forgotten by Israel."[32] Israel must wait until messianic times when, according to this mystical approach, comprehending Torah and perceiving the full splendor of the Kingdom of God will once again be effortless endeavors.

Like the biblical God, Gatsby still hopes for Daisy's return, but Gatsby—like God—returns to his seclusion and relies upon Daisy to seek him, just as God now relies upon Israel so seek Him. As God has retreated further and further from an active role in history, so much so that the "death of God" has famously been propounded as a theology by those such as Dietrich Bonhoeffer,[33] Gatsby likewise dramatically withdrew from Daisy—hence the novel's dark conclusion, in which Gatsby's demise symbolizes the irrevocable withdrawal of God from the sphere of human action. After Gatsby's death and, *mutatis mutandis,* after 1945,[34] God, like Gatsby is even more hidden;[35] Israel, like Daisy, must now assume agency, and may—if they wish—carry on the work of God and Gatsby voluntarily.[36]

More than man seeks God, taught Heschel, God seeks man; this is the essence of Heschelian theotropic theology.[37] Reading *The Great Gatsby* and viewing *Gatsby* through the prism of Heschelian theology can thus help us understand what it means for an inscrutable being to seek an object of desire. Additionally, conceiving of God in anthropopathic terms, as Heschel proposed—believing that God has human emotions—helps elucidate why God's quest to attain Israel's acceptance of the covenant was suffused with such heightened emotion. God's love for Israel and her ancestors, God's jealousy concerning Israel's worship of other gods, and God's anger at Israel's betrayal may only be explicable if one ascribes human emotions to the biblical God. And viewing Gatsby's pursuit of Daisy (particularly as it is portrayed in Luhrmann's adaptation of Fitzgerald's novel) as theologically analogous to the anthropopathic God's pursuit of Israel greatly illuminates what it means to believe in a God with human emotions. One need not adopt Heschelian theology in order to appreciate the pentateuchal narratives—after all, the proliferation of Maimonides's apophatic theology did not prevent generations of Jews from studying the Bible with great ardor—but the consideration of apopathic theology allows for the Bible's literary and cinematic motifs to surface. Reading *The Great Gatsby,* and viewing *Gatsby,* illustrates and adumbrates what Heschel believed to be God's impassioned search for man.

It is Luhrmann's creative contrivance of Gatsby's shattering of the glass that, even more than the film's Jay-Z score, accounts for the undeserved opprobrium that has been heaped upon *Gatsby.* According to the film's detractors, DiCaprio's shattering of the glass—a visual that is conspicuously absent from Fitzgerald's novel and is solely a product of Luhrmann's and writer Craig Pearce's own imaginations—symbolizes Luhrmann's wanton desecration of Fitzgerald's original text. Luhrmann and his crew, critics aver, have corrupted a culturally sacred novel by interpolating imagined scenes and music into the book in order to render it more cinematic. Yet, for a film which has garnered unfair obloquy for taking creative license—and if creative license is not a prerogative of a director charged with adapting a screenplay, for whom is creative license ever sanctioned?—what is remarkable about *Gatsby* is its painstaking faithfulness to Fitzgerald's original work. Save for a few relatively innocuous details—DiCaprio's shattering of the glass in the Plaza Hotel suite, the omission of the scenes involving Gatsby's father, and the situating of Tobey Maguire (Nick) in the sanatorium as a framing device that functions as an etiology for the novel's origins—most of the dialogue is virtual word-for-word transcription from the novel,[38] and so closely resemble Fitzgerald's prose that one could scarcely call the screen-play "adapted"; "lifted" would be a more apt term—especially vis-à-vis Ma-guire's voice-over narrations, most of which are wholesale transcriptions from the novel. However, this description should not imply a judgment; would not literate viewers desire that an adaptation's dialogue approximate the original's actual words as much as possible? Would theatre audiences rather hear Shakespeare's words, or those of a contemporary director swept away with grandiose notions of improving upon the Bard's dialogue? What is striking about *Gatsby* is not its hip-hop sound-tracks (which, it must be noted, are used quite judiciously and strategically—the rumor of the film being a two-hour hip-hop concert is unfounded), but in how little creative license Luhrmann actually exercises. Indeed, it is in its near-sycophantic faithfulness to the original text wherein its cinematic strengths lie. For it is its very unquestionable fidelity to the text that allows *Gatsby* to creatively inter-pret the novel in fresh ways while still preserving its continuity with the original text—which is the essence of *midrash.* [39]

Midrash can loosely be defined as the imaginative interpretive license a tradition bequeaths to its votaries (or that a tradition's heirs assume for them-selves) to generate new meanings from a sacred text. Most scholars assume that midrash is eisegisis disguised as exegesis; a more fitting term for the contemporizing function of midrash is "jurisgenesis." [40] Midrash may also function eisegetically when it "fills in the blanks" of a scriptural story, as it does in appending the legend of God's suspension of Mount Sinai over the heads of the Hebrews; though the legend ostensibly explains and amplifies the story's ambiguous components (what does it mean that the mountain "trembled violently"? (Exodus 19:18)), such a midrash can also be used to interpolate contemporary values and sentiments into the text. For instance, this particular midrash may have been penned to articulate the conscious or unconscious sentiment that covenantal obligations had become such an over-whelming burden for some Jews that they could not have conceived of their ancestors as having willingly entered into the covenant.

In spite of *Gatsby's* uncanny faithfulness to its source, meticulous fidelity to the original text was not Luhrmann's sole concern, and if it had been, the precious element of *midrash* that imbues *Gatsby* with its tactile vitality and contemporary resonance would have been sacrificed to the gods of otiose literality.

Why then did Luhrmann fabricate the scene of DiCaprio shattering the glass and winding up his fist as if to punch Tom? Because perceptive readers of the novel understand that something much more drastic than a mere harsh look must have occurred to definitively drive Daisy away from Gatsby. The rabbis of the Talmud understood that traditional texts are often glaringly lacking; consequently, new, creative interpretations must be read into these texts in order to unearth their concealed yet true meanings. For instance, the rabbis invented the rather cinematic scene of God hoisting Mount Sinai over Israel's heads and exclaiming, "if you shall accept my Torah, it will be for your good; and if not, here will be your burial place"[41] to account for the missing elements in the revelation story, and to explain what had been so frightening about God's approach to Israel at that pivotal moment that could have provoked Israel's idolatrous reversion at Sinai. Luhrmann uses the same poetic license of *midrash* to account for what was so frightening to Daisy about Gatsby's behavior in the Plaza hotel room that could have impelled Daisy to flee back into Tom's arms: only something as intimidating as a fist raised with murderous intent, something as shocking as seeing a glass obliterated with jealous fury, or something as petrifying as having a mountain suspended over one's head in zealous rage, could account for Daisy's sudden volte-face. Luhrmann's unabashed use of such poetic license is indicative that, more than *Gatsby* is Luhrmann's latest splashy, flamboyant feature, *Gatsby* is Luhrmann's filmic midrash of the Fitzgerald novel. Indeed, *Gatsby's* surprisingly muted tone belies the unfair generalization that every Luhrmann film will inevitably be suffused with excessive ostentational[42] exuberance. Luhrmann's and Pearce's limited improvisations bespeak their faithfulness to the spirit (if not the letter) of *The Great Gatsby;* yet they do not hesitate to proffer creative interpretations when the text seems to beg for such readings. In these respects, Luhrmann's *Gatsby* epitomizes the hermeneutical position which holds that valued texts are *supposed* to be interpreted creatively[43] and in accord with the ethos of the times. For example, regarding the traditional Jewish method of reading the Bible, James Kugel has observed that the Bible was never read as a stand-alone text, but has always been read *as it has been interpreted*:

> We like to think that the Bible, or any other text means "just what it says." And we act on that assumption: we simply open a book—including the Bible—and try to make sense of it on our own. In ancient Israel and for centuries afterward, on the contrary, people looked to special interpreters to explain the meaning of the Biblical text. For that reason, the explanations quickly acquired an authority of their own. . . . And so it was this *interpreted* Bible, not just the stories, prophecies, and laws themselves, but these texts as they had, by now been interpreted and explained for centuries that came to stand at the very center of Judaism and Christianity. [44]

In fact, it is *more* faithful to a text to interpret it in ways that allow it to maintain its relevance than to interpret it in ways that narrow its applicability to the era in which it was originally written. It was the biblical hermeneutic of *midrash*—(and the legal hermeneutic of *ḥiddush* [creative interpretation])—interpreting texts imaginatively while concomitantly maintaining painstaking fidelity to the text's words—that allowed each generation of Judaism to embrace change while preserving continuity with its tradition.[45]

As Rabbi Joseph Soloveitchik writes, "[t]he power of creative interpretation (*ḥiddush*) is the very foundation of received tradition."[46] Is depicting Nick Carroway listening to Jay-Z any different than the midrashic depiction of Abraham eating matzah on Passover? Viewed superficially, both portrayals are ludicrous anachronisms; Jay-Z's music did not exist in the Jazz Age any more than the Passover holiday existed in second millennium BCE. Viewed symbolically, however, these portrayals are profoundly true figurative attempts to contemporize texts that we hold dear; such imaginative interpretations aren't meant to be held as literally true, of course, but indicate that the interpreters of these texts believe that these characters still resonate in our age, in our language, and in our cultural milieu.

Luhrmann's original, invigorated *Gatsby* is at once a successful film and a compelling literary interpretation because its fidelity to the novel's words establishes continuity with its source while also fashioning several significant creative interpretations that permit *Gatsby* to resonate with twenty-first century audiences. And it is an instructive film for future directors of literary adaptations who aspire to make their source-works speak to current viewers, for it illustrates that the adaptation will only be successful to the extent to which it is loyal to the source-text's actual words. For a viewer in the theatre in which I attended *Gatsby* to call it an "abomination" is to miss the point— the execrable thing would have been for Luhrmann to exercise no creative license whatsoever and keep the novel confined to the Twenties, thereby implying that *The Great Gatsby* is only capacious enough for a single interpretation, and insinuating that the novel cannot be made to speak in a modern voice. The true test of a text's endurance and worth is whether its meaning can transcend its times and speak to those in other generations, in *their* voices, as *Gatsby* does, and as the Bible continues to do as well.

The vitality of rabbinic midrash and cinematic adaptations of classic literature both illustrate the polysemous qualities of both *Gatsby* and Torah. A well-known rabbinic midrash imagines the Torah to have been given in "seventy languages."[47] This midrash is itself subject to multiple interpretations, but its overriding meaning is that enduring literature should not, and cannot, be limited to a single voice or to a single interpretation. The criterion for greatness in literature is whether it can contain multitudes: depth, layers, and complexity reveal significance, whereas univocal interpretations are harbingers of a text's imminent obsolescence. If a work of literature *can* be limited to a single interpretation, it cannot be great literature.

Luhrmann's faithfulness to the text and concomitant engagement in *ḥiddush* (creative interpretation) is most clearly evident in the film's dénouement. Fitzgerald's indelible closing lines ("So we beat on, boats against the current, borne back ceaselessly into the past") are recited, and in a poignant visual acknowledgement of the written medium upon which this cinematic rendition is based (a literary homage that is not without a soupçon of propaganda from the film's writers), the novel's letters float off of the page and evaporate into the ether, symbolizing that the film was faithful to the words of the novel. Yet, the film is not absolutely faithful to the letter of the novel—the letters levitate off the page and into the purview of a new generation charged with gathering the letters and reconstructing them into new interpretations that are in consonance with each new generation's particular zeitgeist. No closing visual could be more fitting, for it serves as a further visualization of how the film's loyalty to the exact words of Fitzgerald's novel was precisely what allowed Luhrmann to create such an imaginative, contemporary, and revivified *Gatsby*.

NOTES

1. David R. Blumenthal, "Tselem: Toward an Anthropopathic Theology" in *Christianity in Jewish Terms* , Tikva Frymer-Kensky, et al., ed.s (Boulder, CO: Westview Press, 2000), http://js.emory.edu/BLUMENTHAL/image2.html.

2. *The Prophets,* though first published after *God in Search of Man,* is in fact the earlier work, insofar as it is based upon the Ph.D. thesis written by Heschel prior to *God in Search of Man.*

3. Abraham Joshua Heschel, *God in Search of Man: A Philosophy of Judaism* (New York: Farrar, Straus and Giroux, 1955), 136 (emphasis in the original).

4. Jonathan Sacks, *Radical Then, Radical Now: On Being Jewish* (New York: Continuum, 2000), 85.

5. Jon D. Levenson. *Creation and the Persistence of Evil: The Jewish Drama of Divine Omnipotence* (New York: Harper & Row, 1988), 144, emphasis in the original.

6. Most astrophysicists estimate the Big Bang to have occurred 13.7 billion years ago, based upon the Hubble Space Telescope's observations; see, e.g., Raymond Bradley and Norman Swartz, *Possible Worlds: An Introduction to Logic and Philosophy* (Indianapolis: Hackett), 1979.

7. F. Scott Fitzgerald, *The Great Gatsby* (New York: Scribner, 1925), 78.

8. Ibid.

9. Irving Greenberg, *For the Sake of Heaven and Earth: The New Encounter Between Judaism and Christianity* (Philadelphia: Jewish Publication Society, 2004), 155.

10. Ibid.

11. Archibald MacLeish, *Book of Job* (Farmington, CT: First Church of Christ, 1955), 8.

12. Ibid., 9, as cited in Levenson, *The Book of Job in Its Time and In the Twentieth Century,* at 47–48.

13. A mysterious, passive courtship by means of concealment that is suggestive of the Lurianic Kabbalistic doctrine of *tzimtzum* (lit., contraction): God is extremely close to us, but needed to conceal Himself in order to allow create a space within His infinite presence for man to exist. God is concealed, but surrounds us, hoping for us to seek Him, just as Gatsby concealed himself while surrounding Daisy in the hopes that she would seek him.

14. According to classical rabbinic theology, all of God's creation was contingent upon Israel's acceptance of the Torah at Mount Sinai—if Israel manifested her exclusive love for God by willingly entering into the Sinaitic Covenant, God's work would be vindicated; if she refused, God's labors would have been vitiated. (See *Song of Songs Rabba* 1:9, *Pesikta Rabbati* 21, *Midrash Tanḥumah* 1, Babylonian Talmud [hereinafter B.T.] *Shabbat* 88a, cited in Rashi, ad loc. Genesis 1:21, s.v. *"yom hashishi:"* "all of [God's creation] was contingent and dependent upon that sixth day of the sixth of Sivan"—the purported day of the giving of the Torah on Mount Sinai. The *Tanḥumah's* formulation is much more evocative of the dramatic stakes involved in God's proposal to Israel at Sinai: "For the sake of the Torah the world stands . . . God made a condition with the world—if Israel accepts [the Torah (i.e., His proposal to enter

into a covenantal love relationship)], it would be good (i.e., 'everything would be right with the world'); and if not, I will return the world to a state of waste and desolation (the '*tohu vavohu*' of the primordial world of Gen. 1:2)." (*Midrash Tanḥumah,* 1998, 3–4) (Translation of the *Tanḥumah* is mine.) God was prepared to essentially undergo a divine immolation were Israel to reject His proposal.)

15. Ḥoreb is an alternative name for Sinai, and may also function here as a circumlocution for Heaven.

16. Mishna, *Avot* 6:2.

17. Heschel, *God in Search of Man,* 425.

18. In Heschelian theology, theotropism refers to God's search for—or "turning towards"— man (from the Greek *theo* [God], and the Greek *trope* [turn]), and anthropopathism refers to the ascription of human attributes (such as emotions, sensations, and character traits) to God (from the Greek *anthrōpo* [human being] and *pathein* and *pathos* [experience, emotion]).

19. Fitzgerald, *The Great Gatsby,* 98.

20. Additionally, the description of Gatsby's smile—perhaps the most famous smile in American literature—bears the hallmarks of divine omniscience:

> He smiled understandingly—much more than understandingly. It was one of those rare smiles with a quality of eternal reassurance in it, that you may come across four or five times in life. It faced—or seemed to face—the whole external world in an instant, and then concentrated on *you* with an irresistible prejudice in your favor. It understood you just as far as you wanted to be understood, believed in you as you would like to believe in yourself, and assured you that it had precisely the impression of you that, at your best, you hoped to convey. (*The Great Gatsby*, 48)

Only the God of Psalm 33 ("From Heaven the Lord looks down, He sees all mankind. From His dwelling place He oversees all inhabitants of earth. He fashions their hearts all together, He comprehends all their deeds," verses 13–15) would be able to concentrate "on *you*" while simultaneously comprehending "the whole external world in an instant."

21. *The Great Gatsby,* 110–111, (emphasis added). While this chapter's focus is upon the anthropopathic and theotropic motifs in *Gatsby*—theological motifs which are largely Jewish in provenance and application—the Christian theological motifs of incarnation in *Gatsby* should be noted as well.

22. On the possibilities of literature as amenable to anthropopathic interpretation, see, e.g., Michael Fishbane, *Biblical Myth and Rabbinic Mythmaking* (New York: Oxford University Press, 2003). As anthropopathic imagery is certainly evident in biblical literature, this chapter argues that anthropapathic imagery may be implicitly lurking in non-biblical literature as well—or, at the very least, such literature (and such films) are amenable to theological readings.

23. Exodus 24:7; cf. B.T., *Avodah Zarah* 2b, discussing Israel's acceptance of the covenant. (Yet, even that consent was temporary, incomplete, and always subject to Israel's mercurial nature, as will be discussed). Other translations, such as the KJV, translate the Hebrew "*nishmah*" as we will "be obedient." However, I believe the word "hear" more precisely captures the Hebrew "*nishmah,*" whose root [sh-m-a] means hear, not obey. Cf. Sacks, *Covenant & Conversation 5772* (2012), "Ki Tavo—Listening and Law" (explaining the key word "*nishmah*" in Israel's acceptance of God's offer of covenant in light of the recognition that there is "no Hebrew word for 'to obey'"; available at http://www.aishdas.org/ta/5772/kiTavo.pdf).

24. Levenson, *The Book of Job in Its Time and In the Twentieth Century,* 50 Though see Levenson's important qualification, ibid., on how God can—and does—nonetheless *command* love.

25. While Nick's lukewarm, unromantic portrayal of Daisy befuddles readers who attempt to discern precisely what made Daisy so worthy of Gatsby's conquest, the interpretive key to Gatsby's love for Daisy may lie in the non-rational nature of love. God loves Israel in spite of her manifold flaws, recalcitrance, and small size; the nations of the world often looked down upon Israel (to put it mildly), just as Nick often appears to demote Daisy in readers' eyes; yet, since love is in the eye of the beholder, both God and Gatsby subjectively feel that Israel and

Daisy are worthy of their love-conquests, irrespective of objective portrayals of Israel and Daisy.

26. Cf. Levenson, *Creation and the Persistence of Evil,* 144.

27. Ibid., 140–144.

28. Fitzgerald, *The Great Gatsby,* 134.

29. This quote is sometimes attributed to the *Tikkunei Zohar,* but can be more accurately traced to eighteenth-century kabbalist Moses Ḥayim Luzzatto. Alon Goshen-Gottstein, "Encountering Hinduism, in Goshen-Gottstein and Korn, ed.s, *Jewish Theology and World Religions* (Portland, OR: Littman Library, 2012), 270, citing Isaiah Tishby, "God, the Torah and Israel are One: The Source of the Saying in Ramḥal's Commentary on the Idra Rabba' (Heb.), *Kiryat Sefer* 50 (1975): 480–92.

30. B.T., *Shabbat* 127a; Mishna, *Pe'ah* 1:1.

31. Cf. Numbers 21:8.

32. Babylonian Talmud, *Eruvin* 54a.

33. N.B.: the "death-of-God theology is, for the most part, not atheism. Instead, it maintains that the living presence of the real God has vanished . . . all that can fill the gap is man." Levenson, *The Book of Job in Its Time and In the Twentieth Century,* 52.

34. An analogy that is still presented with extreme reluctance, the inadequate qualification of *mutatis mutandis* notwithstanding, for ultimately all analogies to the Holocaust are unjust theoretical appropriations of the tragedy for intellectual purposes, and can serve to trivialize its victims by diminishing the uniqueness of the destruction. Nonetheless, for purposes of this theotropic analogy, this comparison seems both apt as well as necessary to account for Gatsby's death in a way consistent with this particular anthropopathic theological reading.

35. Greenberg, *For the Sake of Heaven and Earth,* 156.

36. On how the darkness of Auschwitz—an undeniable manifestation of the hiddenness of God—necessitates a theological construct in which God's covenant with Israel is now voluntary, see Greenberg, "Voluntary Covenant," I: *Perspectives* (New York: National Jewish Resource Center, 1982).

37. See Heschel, *God in Search of Man* and *The Prophets, passim.*

38. Sensible-minded Fitzgerald devotees will either be heartened or disappointed that Tom's philippic about "the dominant race" needing to subjugate the "Colored Empires" is preserved in its full racist-jingoist splendor. (*The Great Gatsby,* 12–13)

39. N.B.: Any creative license or interpretation cannot simply be characterized as midrash, for such quick-and-easy characterizations often perform a disservice to the sui generis genre of midrash and simultaneously fail to acknowledge the forms of creative adaptation and interpretation that are unique to the literary and cinematic media. This chapter, though, presents midrash as a useful analogical tool through which to understand the hermeneutical scheme of Luhrmann's *Gatsby.* (Others have similarly argued that "midrash allows us to penetrate deep into the film text"; Nathan Abrams, "A Double Set of Glasses: Stanley Kubrick and the Midrashic Mode of Interpretation," in *De-Westernizing Film Studies,* ed.s Saer Maty Ba and Will Higbee [London and New York: Routledge, 2012], 141–151, at142; Udi Lion coined the term "midrash qolnoa" [film midrash] in his comparison of rabbinic exegesis to film; see David C. Jacobsen, "The Ma'ale school: Catalyst for the entrance of religious Zionists into the world of media production," *Israel Studies* 9, no. 1 [2004]: 31–60, at 43.) Moreover, this chapter argues that midrash and creative license in film can be methodologies recognized by literary theory as interpretive readings that address "gaps" in texts—especially in Iser's literary methodology, in which innovation is central to the act of interpretation, and for whom the element of surprise is constitutive of both midrash, literary fiction, and film (see, e.g., Daniel Boyarin, *Intertextuality and the Reading of Midrash* [Bloomington, IN: Indiana University Press, 1994], 139.). On midrash as creative license, see Alfred Louch, "The Genesis of Secrecy: On the Interpretation of Narrative (review of Frank Kermode's *The Genesis of Secrecy: On the Interpretation of Narrative)*" *Philosophy and Literature* 5, no. 2 (1981): 226–232; cf. Jeffrey L. Rubinstein, "From Mythic Motifs to Sustained Myth: The Revision of Rabbinic Traditions in Medieval Midrashim," *Harvard Theological Review* 89 (1996): 131–360. And on movies as midrash, see Alicia Ostriker, "Whither Exodus? Movies as Midrash," *Michigan Quarterly Review* 42:1 (2003).

40. See Robert Cover, "The Supreme Court, 1982 Term—Forward: Nomos and Narrative*"* 97 *Harvard Law Review* 4 (1983): 1–12.

41. B.T., *Shabbat* 88a.

42. My coinage.

43. According to the technique of *d'rash* (creative interpretation), texts are supposed to interpreted creatively. However, *d'rash* does not exhaust the limits of possible hermeneutical techniques. According to one of the other four principal methods of Jewish biblical hermeneutics—the technique of *p'shat* (straightforward interpretation)—texts are also supposed to be interpreted according to their plain, literal meaning as well. Nevertheless, the fact that *d'rash* is one of the four principal interpretative techniques in the Jewish hermeneutical tradition illustrates the extent to which the tradition internalized the imperative of creative interpretation in its pursuit of perpetual spiritual renaissance: "every day they (the Torah and the commandments) should be new in your eyes" (Rashi on Deuteronomy 6:6, s.v. *"Asher anokhi metzav'kha hayom "*).

44. James Kugel, *Traditions of the Bible: A Guide to the Bible As It Was at the Start of the Common Era* (Cambridge, MA: Harvard University Press, 1998), xviii–xix.

45. For example, the Talmudic rabbis prohibited marriages in which a man did not obtain a woman's consent, even though a literal reading of scripture does not grant women this protective right, by basing it upon a textually faithful yet interpretively imaginative reading of the story of Isaac and Rebecca's marriage (Genesis 24). The words of the text state that Rebecca was asked whether she consented to the marriage proposal: "Then they said, 'Let's call the young woman and ask her about it.' So they called Rebecca and asked her, 'Will you go with this man?' 'I will go,' she said." (Ibid., verses 57–58) According to the rabbis, this indicates that marital legitimacy requires a woman's complete consent, even though a straightforward and contextual reading of these verses reveals that Rebecca's family had contracted to marry her to Isaac without her consent (see ibid., verses 50–51) prior to asking her "Will you go with this man?" Interpreting the text in accordance with the spirit of the über-patriarchal ethos in which it was written would have precluded reading such a right into scripture; it was only through the use of *midrash* (in this case, the religious prerogative to formulate a *hiddush* by means of *midrash halakhah* [imaginative legal interpretation], and through the additional creative legal hermeneutic of *asmakhta*) by which the rabbis were able to maintain a tradition's continuity with its source-texts and simultaneously ensure the text's relevancy by lending it interpretations in accord with the ethos of a new era. I am indebted to Blu Greenberg for this observation.

46. Joseph B. Soloveitchik, *Halakhic Man* (trans. Lawrence Kaplan; Philadelphia: The Jewish Publication Society, 1983), 81.

47. *Exodus Rabbah* 5:9.

Chapter Twenty-Four

In *Tree of Life*, Jewish Roots

Terrence Malick's *Tree of Life* has perplexed many viewers. Does it have a message? And if so, what is it trying to communicate?

A beautiful, wondrous, and at times overwhelming film, *Tree of Life* is unmatched in sheer ambition by any film I've seen since Stanley Kubrick's *2001: A Space Odyssey*. It sets out to do no less than explain life, human existence and the universe—and attempts to do so through the prism of a single individual.

That person is Jack O'Brien, whom we see as both "young Jack" and "old Jack." Young Jack is played with remarkable poise and equanimity by Hunter McCracken; watching him hold his own with Brad Pitt (the father) is a delight. Of Adult Jack (Sean Penn), we see only intermittent glimpses at work in a skyscraper-filled metropolis; he reflects on his childhood in an idyllic '50s Texas suburb, raised with two brothers by a well-meaning but occasionally harsh father and a loving but at times doting mother (Jessica Chastain).

If most films resemble a typical novel, with a traditional plot and storyline, *Tree of Life* is more like a discursive, stream of consciousness narrative poem. The movie intersperses straightforward vignettes from Jack's childhood with cosmic images from the Hubble Space Telescope; artistic renderings of tiny cells and vast galaxies; and even an elaborate computer-generated sequence of dinosaurs roaming the young planet. Just as a poem's ambiguous musings convey a mood, these awe-inspiring images evoke Jack's emotional turmoil as he attempts to make sense of his life.

What the 67-year-old Malick does with *Tree of Life*—even if he may not be consciously aware of it—is endorse one of Judaism's most sacred values: the fundamental importance of every single human life. "Whoever destroys a soul, it is considered as if he destroyed an entire world. And whoever saves a life, it is considered as if he saved an entire world." This quote—notably cited in *Schindler's List*—is from the Talmud.[1] If you haven't pondered its meaning before, you will after seeing "Tree of Life."

In juxtaposing images of the Big Bang, star formation and evolution with microscopic views of cells forming and bonding with other cells, the film underlines how a single person—composed of billions of cells in intricate combinations—is as complex as the universe.

The sacredness of the individual is a theme of the Torah portion of Naso. Toward the end of the portion, the Torah lists the gifts donated by the tribal princes to the Mishkan (the Tabernacle). Even though the princes donated identical gifts, the Torah repeats each one of them. Commentators say the point of the repetition is to teach us that in G-d's eyes, each gift—and each prince—was as important as the others.

On a superficial level, the story of every human being is essentially the same: We are born, lose our innocence, age and eventually die. But look deeper and you see that each life is unique, and should be treasured as such.

Sometimes the most complicated things have the simplest explanations. *Tree of Life*, one of the more complex films of recent times, may have a surprisingly simple yet powerful meaning. Each human being is as important as the universe, because each human being is as complex and unique as the universe. Just as our universe was born with the Big Bang, ages, evolves life, and will eventually die (astrophysicists teach us that even the universe is not immortal), so too do we humans. If Malick was trying to deliver a sermon through film, I can't think of a better message to impart.

NOTE

1. Mishnah, *Sanhedrin* 4:5, and Babylonian Talmud, *Sanhedrin*, 37a.

Chapter Twenty-Five

Leonardo DiCaprio, Meet St. Augustine

Leonardo DiCaprio won his long-overdue first Oscar for his astonishing performance in Alejandro González Iñárritu's *The Revenant,* a film that is almost as torturous to sit through as it must have been for the actors to make. Watching *The Revenant* is a feat of film-going endurance for the spectator in a curiously similar manner to how, by all accounts, shooting *The Revenant* was an arduous ordeal for its cast. But what is most curious about all of this is the fact that *The Revenant,* which chronicles the trials and (approximately) twelve labors of a nineteenth-century Herculean American frontiersman, is based on a true story.

In the movie, DiCaprio (Hugh Glass) survives brutal cold, a bear mauling (look away, Stephen Colbert!), attacks from a Native American tribe, and other dreadful depredations, all so that he can live to kill the man who murdered his son. It is much more of an Old Testament ("eye for an eye") than New Testament story ("turn the other cheek"), both in terms of its ethical sensibilities and its unabashed violence; the Book of Numbers grants explicit permission for an "avenger of blood" to kill his relative's murderer, and accidental killers are only spared the wrath of an "avenger of blood" if they flee to a designated City of Refuge and remain there until the death of the high priest. (A peculiar system of criminal justice, you might say, but then again, there were no lawyers or jury duty summons or never-ending appeals back then, so perhaps not everyone would prefer our current system.)

DiCaprio endures all this for our pleasure, and we spectators endure his endurance for our viewing pleasure. But isn't this "pleasure" a bit bizarre? Why do we enjoy these depictions of gruesome violence, suffering, and misery—depictions that no one would wish to suffer himself—that, when portrayed by a talented actor like DiCaprio, become "enjoyable," laudable, and even award-worthy? And what about the fact that there was a real person for whom all of this suffering was *not* fictional? Why would we rather enjoy the fictional portrayal of suffering than seek to alleviate the causes from which such suffering springs? Why would we rather commiserate with the fictional Hugh Glass than spend $15.59 (the price of an adult ticket for *The Revenant* in New York City these days) to ease the agony of those today who are suffering like the actual Hugh Glass?

I am not the first to ask these questions, and if any of these problems have perplexed you as well, rest assured that you're also not the first to have conceptualized these complications. The first person to have put this dilemma into words (the written word, at least) was Saint Augustine of Hippo. In his extraordinary autobiographical work of emotional and spiritual introspection, *The Confessions,* written in about 400 CE, Augustine diagnosed the problem of spectatorial compassion—that is, why is it that we tend to love actors' portrayals of misery when we would never wish such suffering upon ourselves?

As an adolescent, Augustine was like many of us: swayed by passion, recklessly romantic ("I was in love with love" ["*amare amabam*"][1]), and an avid theatergoer; it is safe to assume that an adolescent Augustine transplanted to twenty-first century America would love the movies. But that same Augustine was distinguished by his unparalleled self-awareness, and would have asked himself the same question about the movies that he asked himself about the theater:

> Now, why does a man like to be made sad by viewing doleful and tragic scenes, which he himself could not by any means endure? Yet, as a spectator, he wishes to experience from them a sense of grief, and in this very sense of grief his pleasure consists. What is this but wretched madness? [*Quid est nisi miserabilis insania*?!][2]

If we stop to think about it, it *is* a form of mild insanity to want to experience the grief of Hugh Glass. What sane person would choose this as a form of entertainment, let alone award its portrayer with the highest honor in his field? When DiCaprio finally won his much-deserved Oscar in 2016, he was merely following a long line of actors who have won Oscars by suffering on celluloid for our viewing pleasure. From Maria Falconetti in *The Passion of Joan of Arc* (no Oscar, but her indelible performance set the standard for cinematic suffering) in 1928 to Matthew McConaughey in 2013's *Dallas Buyers Club* to a panoply of actors in between, the Academy loves to award misery (and *Misery,* for which Kathy Bates won an Oscar). Oscars for Adrien Brody (*The Pianist*), Nicholas Cage (*Leaving Las Vegas*), Tom Hanks (*Philadelphia*), and Daniel Day-Lewis (*My Left Foot*) make the message to actors unmistakably clear: if you want to win an Oscar, you must suffer for our pleasure.

Why, then, do Oscar voters and cinephiles love sad cinematic spectacles of suffering and misery? Augustine's answer is that our craving to see suffering comes from a natural impulse we all have to be compassionate. We don't really desire to see such misery—what we really crave is to exercise our innate capabilities for compassion. When we see suffering depicted in a movie, our empathetic itch is scratched, giving us the sensation that we have exercised true empathy. But crying on account of pain experienced by a fictional character is like enjoying a sugary drink: our bodies desire sugar because over hundreds of thousands of years, our bodies learned that fruit—which appeals to our taste-buds in part because of its sugar—is nutritious. Our bodies are programmed to crave sugar, but what our bodies truly desire is not the sugar itself, but the nutrients that are attached to the sugar. Consuming the sugar without the nutrients is thus like expending empathetic emotions on the behalf of fictional characters: these are only superficial satisfactions which ultimately do not satisfy the deeper desires of our bodies (for nutrients) and souls (to extend empathy and compassion to real human beings who are generally suffering).

Should we then not go the movies, or go and try not to cry when we see suffering on celluloid? No, Augustine would say; it is good to remind ourselves from time to time that we possess these deep natural reservoirs of compassion. And—in contrast to Augustine—crying for another reminds us of our innate goodness; as Jean Jacques Rousseau wrote, "in giving man tears, nature bears witness that she gave the human race the softest of hearts."[3] The solution is not to avoid movies which depict suffering, but to go, and perhaps even cry, but to realize that our tears are our psyches signaling to us, saying, "what I really want from you is this: do not leave your emotions in the theater; take them outside to the real world, where it is truly needed."

NOTES

1. Augustine, *Confessions* (trans. Henry Chadwick; New York: Oxford University Press, 1991), 49.

2. Ibid., 35.

3. Jean Jacques Rousseau, *Discourse on the Origin of Inequality* (trans. Maurice Cranston; New York: Penguin, 1984), 103.

Bibliography

Abrams, Nathan. "A Double Set of Glasses: Stanley Kubrick and the Midrashic Mode of Interpretation," in *De-Westernizing Film Studies,* ed. Saer Maty Ba and Will Higbee. London and New York: Routledge, 2012.

Augustine, *Confessions.* Trans. Henry Chadwick; New York: Oxford University Press, 1991.

Bellow, Saul. *Herzog.* New York: Penguin, 1961.

Bloom, Harold. *Genius: A Mosaic of One Hundred Exemplary Creative Minds.* New York: Warner Books, 2002.

———. *How to Read and Why.* New York: Touchstone, 2000.

Blumenthal, David R. "Tselem: Toward an Anthropopathic Theology." *Christianity in Jewish Terms* . Tikva Frymer-Kensky, et al., ed.s. Boulder, CO: Westview Press, 2000.

Boyarin, Daniel. *Intertextuality and the Reading of Midrash.* Bloomington, IN: Indiana University Press, 1994.

Bradley, Raymond, and Norman Swartz. *Possible Worlds: An Introduction to Logic and Philosophy.* Indianapolis: Hackett, 1979.

Brettler, Marc Zvi; Enns, Peter; & Harrington, S.J., Daniel J. *The Bible and the Believer: How to Read the Bible Critically & Religiously.* New York: Oxford University Press, 2012.

Cover, Robert. "The Supreme Court, 1982 Term—Forward: Nomos and Narrative. " 97 *Harvard Law Review* 4 (1983): 1–12.

Dekker, Jeroen J.H. "A Republic of Educators: Educational Messages in Seventieth-Century Dutch Genre painting." *History of Education Quarterly* (1996): 155-182.

Durkheim, Émile. *The Division of Labor in Society* (1893).

———. *Suicide* (1897).

Ebert, Roger. 2003. "Great Movie: Mean Streets," *Rogerebert.com,* December 31, 2003, accessed January 7, 2015. http://www.rogerebert.com/reviews/great-movie-mean-streets-1973.

———. "How I am a Roman Catholic," *Roger Ebert' s Journal,* March 1, 2013, accessed January 7, 2015. http://www.rogerebert.com/rogers-journal/how-i-am-a-roman-catholic.

———. 2011. "An Autumn Afternoon," Accessed September 13, 2013. http://www.rogerebert.com/reviews/great-movie-an-autumn-afternoon-1962.

———. "A Man Escaped," 2011. Accessed December 16, 2013. http://www.rogerebert.com/reviews/great-movie-a-man-escaped-1956.

———. "My Neighbor Totoro," 2011. Accessed January 19, 2020. https://www.rogerebert.com/reviews/great-movie-my-neighbor-totoro-1993.

———. "The Rules of the Game," February 29, 2004. Accessed January 24, 2020. https://www.rogerebert.com/reviews/great-movie-the-rules-of-the-game-1939.

Fishbane, Michael. *Biblical Myth and Rabbinic Mythmaking.* Oxford: Oxford University Press, 2003.

Fitzgerald, F. Scott. *The Great Gatsby.* New York: Scribner, 1925, 2004.

George, Robert P. "The Evangelist" (review of *America's Pastor: Billy Graham and the Shaping of a Nation,* by Grant Wacker), in *The New York Times Book Review,* December 21, 2014, p. 14.

Gibson, Walter S. *Pieter Bruegel and the Art of Laughter.* Berkeley and Los Angeles: University of California Press, 2006.

Gillman, Neil. *Sacred Fragments: Recovering Theology for the Modern Jew.* Philadelphia: Jewish Publication Society, 1990.

Goshen-Gottstein, Alon, and Korn, Eugene, ed.s. "Encountering Hinduism," *Jewish Theology and World Religions.* Portland, OR: Littman Library, 2012.

Greenberg, Irving. *For the Sake of Heaven and Earth: The New Encounter Between Judaism and Christianity.* Philadelphia: Jewish Publication Society, 2004.

———. "Voluntary Covenant." I *Perspectives.* New York: National Jewish Resource Center, 1982.

Hartman, David, with Charlie Buckholtz. 2011. *The God Who Hates Lies: Confronting & Rethinking Jewish Tradition.* Woodstock, VT: Jewish Lights.

Heschel, Abraham Joshua. *God in Search of Man: A Philosophy of Judaism.* New York: Farrar, Straus and Giroux, 1955.

———. *The Prophets.* New York: Harper and Row, 1962.

———. *Who Is Man?* Stanford, CA: Stanford University Press, 1965.

Iser, Wolfgang. *The Act of Reading.* Baltimore: Johns Hopkins University Press, 1978.

Jacobson, David C. "The Ma'ale school: Catalyst for the entrance of religious Zionists into the world of media production." *Israel Studies* 9, no. 1 (2004): 31–60.

Kugel, James. *Traditions of the Bible: A Guide to the Bible As It Was at the Start of the Common Era.* Cambridge, MA: Harvard University Press, 1998.

Levenson, Jon D. *The Book of Job in Its Time and In the Twentieth Century.* Cambridge, MA: Harvard University Press, 1972.

———. *Creation and the Persistence of Evil: The Jewish Drama of Divine Omnipotence.* New York: Harper & Row, 1988.

Louch, Alfred. "The Genesis of Secrecy: On the Interpretation of Narrative (review)." *Philosophy and Literature* 5, no. 2 (1981): 226–232.

Luzzatto, Rabbi Moshe Chaim. *Mesillat Yesharim (The Path of the Just).*

MacLeish, Archibald. *Book of Job.* Farmington, CT: First Church of Christ, 1955.

Maimonides, Moses. *The Guide of the Perplexed.* Trans. Shlomo Pines; Chicago: University of Chicago Press, 1963.

Mann, Thomas. *The Magic Mountain.* Trans. John E. Woods; New York: Knopf, 1995.

Midrash Tanhumah. Mefo'ar edition (Heb.). Bnei Brak, Israel: Or Hahayim Press, 1998.

Milton, John. *Paradise Lost.* New York: Barnes & Noble Classics, 2004.

Neill, Michael. "*Henry V:* A Modern Perspective." In The Folger Library Edition of *Henry V.* New York: Washington Square Press, 1995. 253–278.

Ostriker, Alicia. "Whither Exodus? Movies as Midrash." *Michigan Quarterly Review* 42:1. 2003. Web.

Otto, Rudolph. *The Idea of the Holy, An Inquiry into the Non-rational Factor in the Idea of the Divine and Its Relation to the Rational.* Trans. John W. Harvey; Oxford, 1923.

Plaskow, Judith. 1990. *Standing Again at Sinai: Judaism from a Feminist Perspective.* New York: Harper & Row.

Rousseau, Jean Jacques. *Discourse on the Origin of Inequality.* Trans. Maurice Cranston; New York: Penguin, 1984.

Rubenstein, Jeffrey L. "From Mythic Motifs to Sustained Myth: The Revision of Rabbinic Traditions in Medieval Midrashim." *Harvard Theological Review* 89 (1996): 131–360.

Sacks, Jonathan. *Radical Then, Radical Now: On Being Jewish.* New York: Continuum, 2000.

———. *Covenant & Conversation 5772.* "Ki Tavo—Listening and Law," 2012. Online publication; available at http://www.aishdas.org/ta/5772/kiTavo.pdf.

———. "Noach: True Morality." *Covenant & Conversation,* 2012.

Sarna, Nahum M. *Understanding Genesis: The World of the Bible in the Light of History.* New York: Schocken, 1970.

Schwartz, Howard. *Tree of Souls: The Mythology of Judaism.* New York: Oxford University Press, 2007.

Scott, A.O. "Between Earth and Heaven." *New York Times,* 3 October 2014.

Seeskin, Kenneth *No Other Gods: The Modern Struggle Against Idolatry.* West Orange, NJ: Behrman House, 1995.

Simon-Shushan, Moshe. *Stories of the Law: Narrative Discourse and the Construction of Authority in the Mishnah.* New York: Oxford University Press, 2012.

Soloveitchik, Joseph B. *Halakhic Man.* Trans. Lawrence Kaplan. Philadelphia: The Jewish Publication Society, 1983.

———. Agency [*Sh'liḥut*]," in *Yemei Zikaron* (Heb.). Aliner Library; WZO, Dept. of Torah Education & Culture; Jerusalem: Orot, 1986.

Sontag, Susan. "The Death of Tragedy," *Against Interpretation and Other Essays.* New York: Farrar, Straus and Giroux, 1961.

Thoreau, Henry David. *Walden.* New York: Barnes & Noble Classics, 2003.

Tishby, Isaiah. "God, the Torah and Israel are One: The Source of the Saying in Ramḥal's Commentary on the Idra Rabba' (Heb.), *Kiryat Sefer* 50, 1975.

Wallace, David Foster. *Both Flesh and Not: Essays.* New York: Little, Brown and Company, 2012.

———. *Infinite Jest.* New York: Little, Brown and Company, 1996.

Walton, John H. *The Lost World of Adam and Eve: Genesis 2–3 and the Human Origins Debate.* Downers Grove, IL: InterVarsity Press, 2015.

Williams, Chris, ed. *The Richard Burton Diaries.* New Haven: Yale University Press, 2012.

Woolf, Virginia. *The Common Reader.* Ed. Andrew McNeillie; New York: Harcourt Brace Jovanovich, 1984.

Index of Films Referenced

Index

About the Author

Daniel Ross Goodman is a writer, rabbi, and scholar from western Massachusetts. He has published in numerous academic and popular journals, magazines, and newspapers, including the *Wall Street Journal, Journal of Religion & Film*, the *Journal of Jewish Ethics,* and the *Harvard Divinity Bulletin*. He currently lives in New York, where he is a Ph.D. candidate at the Jewish Theological Seminary of America. His first novel, *A Single Life,* was published in 2020.